CREATING EDUCATION THROUGH RESEARCH:

a Global Perspective of Educational Research for the 21st Century

Michael Bassey

Kirklington Moor Press in conjunction with the British Educational Research Association

Kirklington Moor Press: The Cottage, The Moor, Kirklington, Newark, NG22 8NQ, England
British Educational Research Association: BERA Office, 15 St John Street, Edinburgh, EH8 8JR, Scotland

© Michael Bassey 1995

First published in 1995

British Library Cataloguing in Publication Data. A catalogue record for this book is available from the British Library.

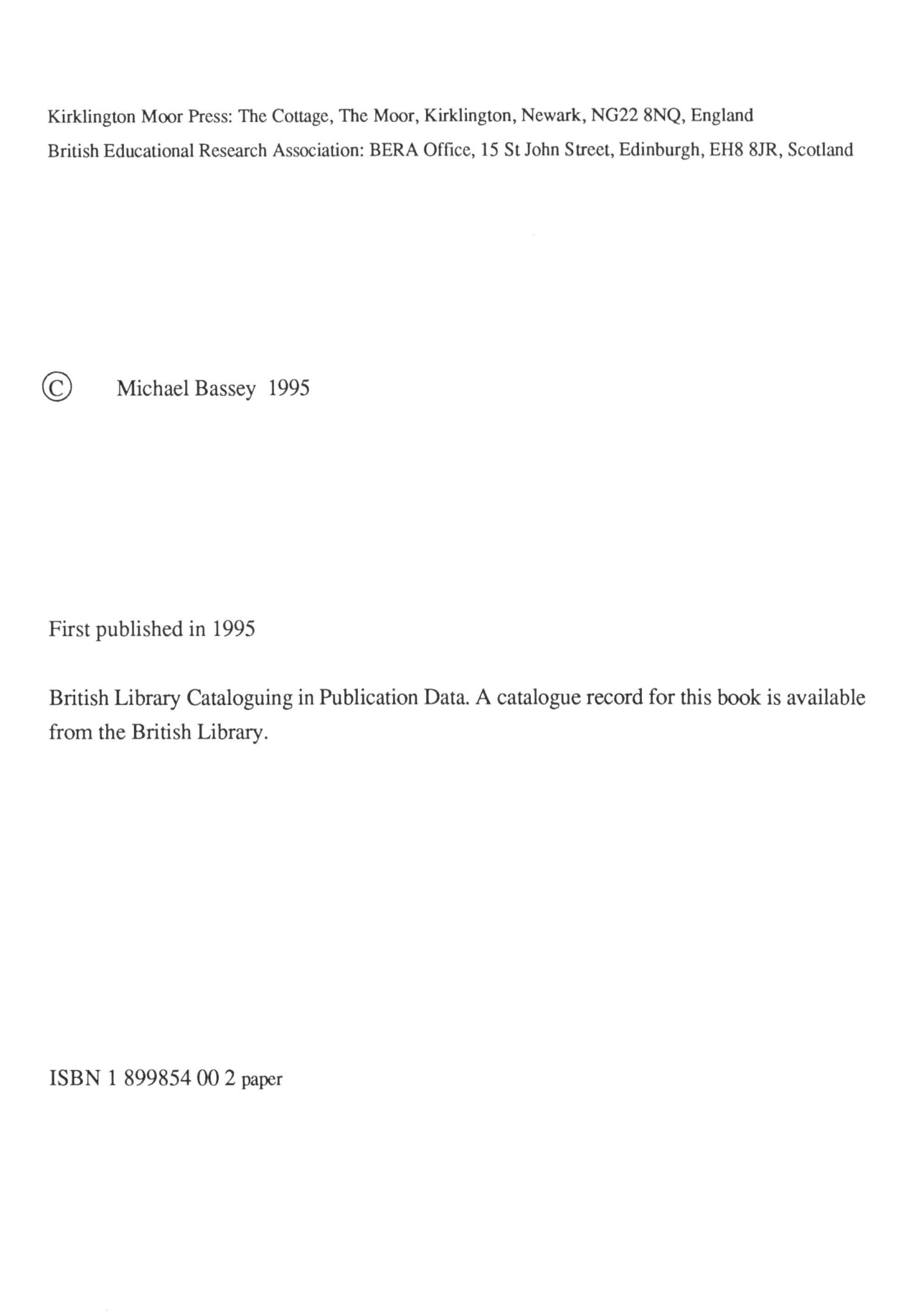

ISBN 1 899854 00 2 paper

CONTENTS

	Foreword by Barry Troyna	iv
	Introduction	v
Chapter One	ON THE NATURE OF SOCIAL RESEARCH	1
Chapter Two	ON THE POLITICS OF RESEARCH IN EDUCATION	18
Chapter Three	ON THE KINDS OF RESEARCH IN EDUCATIONAL SETTINGS	32
Chapter Four	ON THE PROCESS OF RESEARCH IN EDUCATION	53
Chapter Five	ON THE WRITING OF RESEARCH IN EDUCATION	63
Chapter Six	ON SEARCH FOR GENERALISATIONS	86
Chapter Seven	ON STUDY OF SINGULARITIES	109
Chapter Eight	ON QUALITY IN RESEARCH IN EDUCATION	118
Chapter Nine	ON TRIVIAL PURSUITS AND SIGNIFICANT INSIGHTS	126
	Endpiece	138
	References	143
	Names Index	148
	Subject Index	149

FOREWORD

This is an ambitious book. In his determination to go beyond providing yet another text outlining the 'nuts and bolts' of doing research, Michael Bassey has confronted head-on some of the most contentious themes associated with research in educational settings. As a former President of BERA and now its General Secretary, he is well-placed to take on such a daunting task. He is, for instance, not afraid to address the conceptual, epistemological and ethical issues in this area of enquiry. Nor does he shy away from problems of definition, the politics or, indeed, the criteria by which we might assess the quality and relevance of research in education. These are provocative issues; but such a reflexive analysis of this genre of social research is timely, as recent critiques of the enterprise of 'educational research' and the current proliferation of seminars on its future clearly testify.

Creating Education Through Research, then, is a stimulating, controversial and, above all, passionate book. It is intended to and, I believe, succeeds in, provoking discussion about the core issues in this area of enquiry. It could become an important resource for researchers, teachers and students committed to understanding further this complex field of study.

Barry Troyna
Institute of Education
University of Warwick

****

INTRODUCTION

****

DISCOVERIES OF THE OBVIOUS

When I first came into the world, it was obvious that there were authorities and that they knew what they were doing. They told me what to do and what not to do; they told me what was right and what was wrong. Usually I followed their directions. The discovery of these authorities was my first discovery.

Discovery 2 was that the authorities whom I had followed did not always know what they were doing and did not have all the answers. At first I was shocked, then I was pleased. I felt that as soon as I could escape from their tyranny I would be free. It was clear to me that any opinion is as good as any other, mine included. It was time to move into the real world and express my opinions, not theirs.

Discovery 3 came when I moved into the real world as a self-opinionated being and walked smack into a plate-glass wall of a new tyranny - of fact. I was confounded by the complexity of the real world and began to struggle hard to give it meaning. I met others who engaged in the same struggle and I met major differences of opinion among them.

Discovery 4 was that of the plethora of opinions about this real world, not every opinion was as good as any other; indeed some were no good at all. I began to forge intellectual tools for assessing opinions, such as questions like: 'Is it in accord with the evidence? Is it logical? Is it based on respect for persons?'

My fifth discovery was that I am not a watcher of the world, but an actor in it. I have to make decisions and some of them have to be made now. I cannot say, 'Stop the world and let me get off for a bit, I want to think some more before I decide'. Given differences of opinion among reasonable people, I realise that I cannot be sure that I am making the 'right' decisions. Yet because I am an actor in the world, I must decide. I must choose what I believe in and own the consequences.

My most recent discovery is research. If I reflect on some of my actions, analyse why I did what I did and what the consequences were for others, seek criticism from colleagues, read what others have done in similar circumstances, and test out my ideas by searching for evidence, I believe my judgement improves and so, in the heat of the moment when there is little time to think, I make better decisions. It may sound ambitious, but that is my credo.

(Adapted and developed from Perry 1978)

INTRODUCTION

This book is addressed to the community of scholars and students who conduct research into education. They are mainly in universities and research institutes throughout the world. The book explores the nature of research in education, reflects on what it is, analyses its processes, challenges its present scope, and is enthusiastic about its potential future. Overall it is a polemic about the role that I believe research in education could take in the 21st century.

Social research, including research in education, is more than an elegant and self-correcting way of extending and satisfying people's curiosity about themselves and their fellows. It is also a way of safeguarding democracy by ensuring that government of the people, by the people, for the people, is based on rational, critical and humane exploration of what has happened and what is happening, and creative thinking about what could happen in the future.

To the casual reader of research reports, and perhaps for some researchers, this may sound exaggerated and over-ambitious. Philosophers may ask whether it is a descriptive definition (of what is the case) or a prescriptive definition (of what the writer hopes for) and, of course, I must admit to the latter.

Research in education is a complex tangle of beliefs, aims, methods, languages, and intellectual structures. The first purpose of this book is to survey this tangle, to tease out its components, and to suggest a coherent framework in which research in educational settings is sub-divided into educational research, sociological research in education, psychological research in education, philosophical research in education and historical research in education. This firmly establishes the credibility and value of educational research as a free-standing member of the social sciences. I tackle this in Chapters One to Three.

Secondly, the book shows ways in which the process of enquiry and the writing of findings can be sharpened. To the same end the problem of generalisation of research findings and the merit of studies of singularities is discussed. These ideas, developed in Chapters Four to Eight, all point to ways in which the quality of educational research can be enhanced. Quality is discussed in terms of adventureness in the choice of topic, elegance of the process and worthwhileness of the product.

Finally the book considers the agenda of educational research and, in rejecting trivial pursuits conducted by individuals, points to the wide range of significant issues that the idea of a learning society can expect educational researchers to address. Country by country the formal education systems of the world deserve the focused intelligence of researchers striving to improve policy and practice. Globally the world has a need for empirical, reflective and creative educational research into learning how to prevent famine, war, environmental pollution, over-population, resource depletion, extinction of wild-life species, and disruption of ecological systems.

Thus the book establishes the credibility of educational research, suggests ways of enhancing its quality, and focuses attention on its future agenda. Much of the source material is drawn from the United Kingdom, but the issues discussed transcend political boundaries and are international in scope.

Looking back I realise that I have been working on this analysis and synthesis for nearly a quarter of a century and, in wondering where the ideas come from, realise that they have slowly come together as a result of many research events in which I have had the privilege to take part. These include: working with research students and particularly MEd students at Trent Polytechnic, which became Nottingham Polytechnic and then the Nottingham Trent University; examining research theses and masters assignments and dissertations at a number of English universities; serving on the Council for National Academic Awards (now abolished) committee for approving research degree proposals in Education; serving as a consultant to the UK Economic and Social Research Council Training Board for the recognition of Education departments (1991 and 1992); serving on the UK Higher Education Funding Councils' Research Assessment Exercise panel for Education (1992); refereeing papers for several journals; and, especially, participating in the conferences and Executive Council of the British Educational Research Association.

The essence of these events has been dialogue and here I would like to acknowledge the encouragement and stimulus to creative and reflective thought that I have obtained from conversation with so many researchers and teachers. Only a few are cited in the text, and then only when their empirical findings are being used as evidence in argument, for in my view creative and reflective writing must be expressed as the responsibility of the writer and not sandbagged (a term used in Chapter Five) by names. Some will perhaps be surprised that I thank them and some may be displeased at the synthesis of ideas that I have made from our conversation. May I be forgiven for those whom I have forgotten. My sources of inspiration, the people to whom I owe much, include: Clem Adelman, Mauri Ahlberg, Stephen Ball, Penny Bassey, Neville Bennett, Sally Brown, Robert Burgess, Tom Baum, Rosemary Deem, John Elliott, Caroline Gipps, Michael Golby, Mark Hadfield, Sheila Hall, Nina Hatch, David Hamilton, Wynne Harlen, Mary Hayes, David Hustler, Pam Lomax, John Nisbet, Peter Ovens, Stewart Ranson, Jean Rudduck, Derek Sharples, Brian Simon, Helen Simons, Lawrence Stenhouse, Barry Troyna, Peter de Vriess, Gwen Wallace, Gaby Weiner, Jack Whitehead, Ted Wragg, Alan Wright, Mick Youngman.

INTRODUCTION

The title 'Creating Education through Research' was also the title of my presidential address to the British Educational Research Association in 1991 and I am grateful to the editor of the *British Educational Research Journal* for permission to reproduce sections of it. Likewise I must thank the editors of *Research Intelligence, The Times Educational Supplement, The Higher,* and the *Oxford Review of Education* for the opportunity to use material originally published by them.

Throughout the world the educational research community is in ferment. Most governments have come to believe that educational development is a requirement for economic growth and that perhaps research can promote development. Usually this realisation is accompanied by parsimony with funding, but nevertheless educational researchers are beginning to overcome the lethargy of recent decades and are gaining significant insights in fields of enquiry such as assessment, equal opportunities, active learning and school effectiveness. Whether this surge of activity is the result of being goaded by government in a 'discourse of derision' (as has happened in the UK), or is a consequence of enhanced international contacts through electronic communication, or is simply excitement at the prospect of the next millennium (can researchers be so emotional?), the fact is that educational researchers are on the march. I hope that this book will offer sustenance to some and a guide to others, but for all will give a stimulus to raising the quality, credibility and impact of educational research in order to make the world a better place to live in.

To repeat the final sentence: creating education through research is not just the title of a book; it is an imperative for democratic societies in a free world.

Michael Bassey
July 1995

Chapter One

ON THE NATURE OF SOCIAL RESEARCH

Sections

1.	A DEFINITION OF RESEARCH	1
2.	A TOPOGRAPHY OF SOCIAL RESEARCH	4
	2.1 Three realms	5
	2.2 Three categories	6
	2.3 Two kinds of enquiry of empirical researchers	7
	2.4 Three different audiences	9
	2.5 Three levels of communication	10
3.	THE DEEP STRUCTURE OF SOCIAL RESEARCH IN THE 1990s	11
	3.1 The positivist research paradigm	12
	3.2 The interpretive research paradigm	13
4.	THE ETHICS OF SOCIAL RESEARCH	15
	4.1 Respect for persons	15
	4.2 Respect for truth	16
	4.3 Respect for democratic values	16

Although the book as a whole is about educational research, this chapter takes a broader view and discusses the nature of social research in general, which I take to embrace education, social work, psychology, sociology, anthropology, criminology, management studies, and many other areas of academic enquiry such as police studies, transport studies and opinion polling where human behaviour is the major variable. This broadening is deliberate, for I consider that for too long educational research has been isolated from related subjects whose practitioners debate many of the same methodological issues that perplex educationists. A sharing of insights amongst social scientists would profit everyone.

The style of much of this book is didactic and authoritative. Here I utter definitions and classify ideas as though they are carved in stone: this is what is meant by xxx; there are three categories of yyy and two of zzz. [Somebody said to me recently during a lecture: 'There are two kinds of people, those who say there are two kinds of people, and those who don't. You seem to be one of the former.'] As a teacher I oscillate between letting people invent their own wheels and telling them about mine. Here I'm doing the latter. Only rarely shall I give the pedigree of ideas I am writing about. This is for two reasons. First because I believe that to put a footnote to each assertion would so confound the text that it would be difficult to read. Secondly because although I could trace a few of the assertions back to their source there would be many others whose origin is now lost in the tumultuous sea of ideas in which I have floundered for many years and often been near drowned, to escape by constructing a raft which is my present understanding of research as expressed here! In defence of this style I would say to the reader, as I have said many times to my students, 'If these ideas make sense to you then use them until you find something better; if they don't make sense forget them.'

* * * * *

1. A DEFINITION OF RESEARCH

It may seem pedantic to suggest that in order to carry out research we need to be sure what research is, but it is often helpful to start with a definition. This is particularly true of social research because, as this chapter will show, it comes in many forms. In my experience this definition is acceptable to most people; it arises from the teaching of Lawrence Stenhouse:

> **Research is systematic, critical and self-critical enquiry which aims to contribute to the advancement of knowledge.**

It is worth examining the parts of this definition in some detail, as follows.

Chapter One ON THE NATURE OF SOCIAL RESEARCH

Enquiry

Research is enquiry conducted for some clearly defined purpose; it is not a random amassing of data. It entails an attempt, which may not be achieved, to get the answers to questions, for example 'what is happening here', 'how can this problem be tackled' or 'is this hypothesis correct?'

Systematic

In pursuit of the enquiry, data are collected and analysed in a regular way which is underpinned by a rationale or theory. Researchers are expected to record each item as far as possible in such a way as to ensure that it can be checked over.

Critical

The data which are collected are subject to close scrutiny by the researcher in attempts to ensure that they are as accurate as necessary and that each item is what it purports to be. Likewise the interpretations, explanations and conclusions are subject to questioning which challenges them logically and rationally. The data and its analysis need to be handled in ways which the research community judges to be ethical. If the data are a sample of something, the researcher strives to ascertain how representative they are of the population sampled. Researchers are expected to examine critically their data to ensure trustworthiness.

Self-critical

Researchers are expected to be self-critical of the decisions made by themselves in pursuit of the enquiry. They are expected to examine critically their methods of collecting data, of analysing them, and of presenting findings.

The advancement of knowledge

An essential characteristic of research is that the enquiry should aim to increase knowledge. Its purpose should be to make a claim to new knowledge: to tell someone something that they didn't know before. Initially the result of an enquiry is personal knowledge for the researcher, and where research is being used by the individual to try to improve his or her practice, as in some forms of action research, that may be as far as it will go. More commonly however the expectation is that the researcher will publish the findings to as wide an audience as may benefit from the new knowledge. As the 19th century scientist Michael Faraday put it, 'work, finish, publish'.

Knowledge

'Knowledge' means understandings about events and things and processes: it includes descriptions, explanations, interpretations, value orientations, as well as knowledge of how these can be arrived at: in other words it includes knowledge that something is the case and knowledge how to do something: it includes theory-in-the-literature as well as the personal theory of individuals which has not been articulated in writing.

Some would change the phrase 'advancement of knowledge' to 'advancement of knowledge and wisdom', where *wisdom* is taken to be the disposition and ability to act on knowledge.

* * * * *

Two infant children (or, as we say now in England, two children working at key stage one) were discussing the age of their teacher. 'I know how we could find out', said one. 'How?, asked the other. 'Look in her knickers, 'cos in my knickers there's a label that says "for ages 5 to 6"'. This story draws attention to many aspects of social research. Would extrapolation from 5 to 30, or 40, or 50 be valid? How would the observation be made? Would this be ethical? Is there an easier way of making the enquiry? Perhaps most important of all are these questions: What do you seek to know that you didn't know before? Why do you want to know? Who will you tell? How will this change the world?

Forget the story but look again at the last of these questions. Let me assert, right from the start, that the demanding and rigorous procedures of research should not be wasted on trivial pursuits. Social research should be about understanding and improving the world!

* * * * *

2. A TOPOGRAPHY OF SOCIAL RESEARCH

I propose to draw a map of the land of social research as I see it. It is a land of widely different regions with people of different cultures, different aspirations, and sometimes different languages that are hardly understood by others; a land of plateaux that are easy to traverse and of mountains that are difficult to climb; a land where in places the climate is conducive to research, but elsewhere is arid and researchers need to work hard to scratch findings from the soil. It is a land inhabited by professional people who belong to tribes with names such as sociologists, psychologists, anthropologists, economists, historians, educationists, and others. Sometimes there are rivalries between the tribes and sometimes fights break out within the tribes, but overall this is a land where 'systematic and critical inquiry' is written over every doorway: all are engaged in the pursuit of new knowledge.

This land of research is categorised by three realms, three categories of work, two kinds of empirical enquiry, three different audiences, and three levels of communication.

2.1 Three realms: empirical research, reflective research and creative research

Empirical research means the kind of research where data collection is centre stage: research where questions are asked of people, observations made of events, and measurements taken of artefacts by researchers using predominantly their own eyes and ears and brains to ensure that data are systematically collected by strict procedures, critically analysed, interpreted and conclusions drawn. There is a tendency for empirical researchers to see this as the only form of research, but I argue that there are two other forms.

Reflective research is a term to describe systematic and critical thinking in which the findings of empirical research, often carried out by others, are the starting point for critical review and logical argument about social issues. Many articles in the literature are of this form. Fieldworkers in the sweat and toil of data collecting may castigate these writings as the work of armchair theorists, but this is no more than a replay of the age-old battle between doers and thinkers: both play essential parts in the advancement of knowledge.

Creative research is the devising of new systems, the development of novel solutions, and the formulation of new ideas, which is based on systematic and critical enquiry into existing knowledge, but which has yet to be subjected to the rigorous evaluation of empirical research. This is a realm of enquiry which is often excluded from research listings, but in my view, provided that it is carried out with system and criticism, it can justly be described as research.

My reason for identifying these three realms of social research is to emphasise the notion that all enquiries which are conducted systematically and critically in order to make a claim to knowledge are research. It follows that the army of social researchers is a large one.

In practice, of course, the three realms overlap: the boundaries are somewhat vague. For example, the empirical researcher is bound to engage in some reflection in order to draw conclusions, and the reflective researcher has to read the literature in order to obtain data to think about. Likewise the novel approach adopted by an empirical researcher, and the new insight which develops in the writing of a reflective researcher, overlaps with the creative realm. Nevertheless these overlaps are usually small and so it is often possible to categorise a piece of research as lying predominantly within one of these realms.

2.2 Three categories: theoretical research, evaluative research, and action research

Theoretical research: enquiry carried out in order to understand
This category of research work has the purpose of trying to describe, interpret or explain what is happening without making value judgements or trying to induce any change. The researchers are trying to portray the topic of their enquiry as it is. The aim is to give theoretical accounts of their topic - perhaps of its structures, or processes, or relationships - which link with existing theoretical ideas. They are not seeking to evaluate it and they strive to investigate without disturbing. Of course, others may use the findings to initiate change, but the researchers themselves aim to complete the enquiry without changing the situation. This work is usually carried out by 'outsiders', ie people who are not engaged directly in the social practice under study. Before the 1980s this was seen by most academics as the only category of research work.

Evaluative research enquiry carried out in order to understand and evaluate
A second category of research work is done by evaluators. Like those who seek to understand, the evaluators also are trying to describe, interpret or explain what is happening, but in doing so they are setting out to make value judgements, or to portray events so that others may make value judgements, about the worthwhileness of the topic. The expected endpoint is that someone will use their findings to decide whether or not to try to induce change. This work may be carried out by 'outsiders' or by 'insiders'.

Action research enquiry carried out in order to understand, evaluate and change
A third category of research work is carried out by action researchers. They are trying to induce beneficial change. Of course, in order to do this it is first necessary to understand what is happening and to evaluate it, then to introduce change and evaluate the new situation. They are using systematic and critical enquiry in attempts to improve the practical situation. It is usually carried out by 'insiders', ie people who are directly engaged in the practice under study.

Insiders and outsiders
The term 'insider' means a practitioner engaging in research on some aspect of his or her own practice, while an 'outsider' is a researcher from the outside.

Mobility between the categories
Referring to 'categories' of research work does not imply that there is no mobility between the categories, for obviously a researcher may act at one time as a theoretician, at another time as an evaluator and at another as an action researcher.

2.3 Two kinds of enquiry of empirical researchers: the search for generalisations and the study of singularities

The *search for generalisations* and the *study of singularities* represent two quite different forms of research enquiry and probably constitute the most important dichotomy in social research. The search for generalisation requires the investigation of large populations, usually studied by appropriate sampling, and by intention leads to statements which can be used to *predict* what will occur in other situations. The study of a singularity can be investigation of something quite small, for example a researcher reported on the reading strategies engaged in by one infant teacher during a four minute period of observation. Clearly this cannot be used to predict probabilities, but if it can be *related* to other situations, it may be valuable. Both of these forms of research entail systematic, critical and self-critical enquiry which aims to contribute to the advancement of knowledge, but the divide between them is so great that until recently the practitioners of the former were inclined to deny that the latter is research. ('How can you make a generalisation when N =1', they said, failing to recognise that the researchers studying singularities were not trying to make generalisations from single studies.) The report of the study of a singularity is often called a case study.

To start with definitions, this is how these terms can be used:

> *A study of a singularity is research into particular events.*
>
> *A search for generalisation is research leading to a statement which collates evidence of particular events, and extrapolates that evidence to predict the occurrence of similar events.*

A trivial example provides a first illustration. Consider this conclusion which might arise from a study of the events taking place early in the school day in a particular set of schools:
> In every one of these schools, throughout the period of this study, early in the school day an attendance register was taken to see which pupils were absent.

This refers to a set of particular events and is thus described as a study of a singularity.

The same research data could lead to a generalisation, which would be expressed like this:

> In every school in this *country*, early in the school day an attendance register *is* taken to see which pupils *are* absent.

In order to make this generalisation, its author would need to be confident that it was reasonable to extrapolate from the sample of schools studied to the whole country and also would need to be confident that it was reasonable to predict that this is an ongoing account.

The conclusion of the above *study of a singularity* - events in a particular set of schools - is phrased in terms of the particular schools studied. The conclusion of the *search for a generalisation* goes beyond the particular schools studied, it also predicts that this same event happens in all schools in the country. The italics in the quotations emphasis the difference.

A singularity has a temporal and spatial boundary which is local, not general: it describes, analyses, explains, interprets, perhaps seeks to justify, something which occurred at a particular place (or set of places) and at a particular time (or set of times). The generalisation also, inevitably, has a boundary, but this is not local; predictions of events beyond the locality and time studied are made.

Because a singularity is local, it can be described in considerable detail: the above example of a singularity is trivial because it is hardly using this form of research effectively. Suppose that instead of visiting a number of schools and noting whether registers were taken early in the day, the researchers selected a few schools and reported in some detail how the register was taken. They might find, for example, that in one case each pupil's name was called out by the teacher and the pupil answered 'Yes Miss', while in a second case the teacher insisted on the response 'Yes Miss Brown'; in a third case the pupils might have allotted numbers and the teacher calls out 'Number 1, please start' and each pupil, in sequence, then calls out his or her number so that the room echoes to '2', '3', '4', '5', etc. The researchers might record the teacher's reasons for using a particular system and the pupils' views of it. They might find, for example, that although the institutional function of register-taking is to ascertain who is absent, it also serves an important social function in signalling to the class that work is about to begin and gives them a few moments to settle into an appropriate frame of mind. The point of this study would be to make available to other teachers ideas about this activity, which they might relate to their own register-taking practice and perhaps improve it.

By contrast a generalisation entails much less detail. Suppose that the outcome of observation in a representative sample of schools is expressed by the researchers in the form of this generalisation:

> Register taking using the numbering system requires about half the time required by the calling-out-names system.

Any teacher reading this could apply the prediction to his/her class and, if time saving was worthwhile, act accordingly.

Researchers working within a singularity will choose their data sources on the ground of particular interest - perhaps novelty, or excellence, or because it is their own work which they are interested in investigating. They will hope that their audience can *relate* the research report to their own situation. ('Relating' implies that although one situation is different from another, there are sufficient similarities for situations to be related to each other.) By contrast, researchers seeking to announce a generalisation will choose their data sources on the grounds of being representative of the whole population for which a research report is to be made. They will hope that their audience can *generalise* the research report to their own situation. ('Generalising' implies that one situation is similar to another, hence a finding in one place can be transferred directly to another.)

Stenhouse described these two research forms as 'the study of samples' and 'the study of cases'. They are discussed in more detail in Chapter Six and Chapter Seven.

It is almost inevitable that small scale research - such as a student preparing an assignment, special study, or dissertation - will be in the form of study of a singularity. To formulate valid generalisations requires greater resources than can usually be mobilised by individual students. My quarrel with many contemporary studies by students is that they attempt to formulate generalisations as a result of research into singularities. Beware!

2.4 Three different audiences for research findings: researchers, practitioners, and policy-makers

This is probably the least recognised division, which is unfortunate for it explains some of the tensions which can exist between those who engage in some of the kinds of research described above.

Other researchers as audience
Research is a cumulative activity in which theoretical findings need to be readily available for other researchers to draw on. Hence the research community is one vital audience. Papers and books written for this audience need to be written in an academic style which embeds new claims to knowledge in the existing knowledge by frequent cross-referencing to the literature.

Technical language appropriate to the enquiry may be used, on the grounds that those who will use the writing will be familiar with it. Sufficient detail is needed to substantiate the claim to knowledge to the satisfaction of other academics. In consequence, what is written for an audience of researchers may not be easily comprehended by either practitioners or policy-makers.

Practitioners and policy-makers as different audiences with different needs

Practitioners are the teachers, social workers, managers, administrators, police officers, health workers, etc who expect that research will aid their practice in working with pupils, clients, customers, staff, members of the public, etc. The policy-makers are the members of Parliament, civil servants, local authority officers, and indeed the general public, who expect that research will aid the making of policy for the future direction of society. Practitioners work with small numbers of people, where hopefully the idiosyncrasy of every individual can be responded to. Policy-makers work with large populations, where the average characteristics of the majority are the focus of concern and the interests of minorities may be too many and too complicated to warrant detailed consideration. Thus the kind of new knowledge which practitioners seek, as an audience, is that which gives detailed accounts that they can relate to their working situations - ie studies of singularities. But the kind of new knowledge which policy-makers seek is quite different, they need simplified accounts of average situations - ie generalisations.

2.5 Three levels of communication: the personal, the informal interactive, and the formal dissemination levels

As a matter of speculation consider the idea that researchers have three levels of engaging in criticism in relation to other researchers.

Level One is the *personal level*, where one is working more or less alone in designing an enquiry, collecting data, analysing and interpreting it, drawing tentative conclusions, and reflecting on the process and outcomes. At this level each researcher talks to the self and this may often provide the most virulent critiques of the work.

Level Two is the *informal interactive level* where the enquiry is shared with selected others (orally or in writing) for critical appraisal of its meaningfulness. In my view this is often a neglected level, researchers jumping from One to Three without the benefit of peer critique. It isn't necessarily the fault of the researcher, it may be that colleagues can't spare the time to think deeply about the work, or are reluctant to challenge it.

Level Three is the *formal dissemination level* where an account of the enquiry and its findings is published in the literature: although still open to critical challenge, the findings tend to be taken by readers as fact. In my view this is the level where there is much room for improvement. Too much reporting of educational research is poorly expressed, a matter to be discussed further in Chapter Five.

* * * * *

This may look like a neat and tidy account of social research, but in truth it is only topographical, an account of the surface, the view of the landscape observer. What lies underneath? What of the underlying structures of hard rock and soft rock, of anticlines and synclines, of faults and intrusions, of pockets of molten rock waiting to be expelled in volcanic eruptions? I refer to the belief systems which underlie our actions.

* * * * *

The clinical professor was lecturing on diabetes. He was authoritative, dominant, and not-to-be-argued-with. A dozen students were seated around the demonstration bench on which stood a beaker of yellow liquid. 'Ladies and gentlemen, observation is everything. If it hadn't been for the observation that flies were attracted to a trickle of urine down the leg of a laboratory bench which had been made by a dog whose pancreas had been removed, we would not have our present test of looking for sugar in the urine of suspected diabetics. I repeat, observation is everything. Now please do as I do to reinforce this point.' He dipped a finger into the yellow liquid and appeared to taste it. The students squirmed, but he was not-to-be-argued-with. They dipped their fingers, tasted them, and one, seeking credit from the professor, said 'Yes sir, it's sweet! ' 'You did not observe carefully,' came the reply, 'look again. I dipped one finger into the liquid, but licked another.'

What misunderstandings do we have because we fail to challenge our senses?

* * * * *

3. THE DEEP STRUCTURE OF SOCIAL RESEARCH IN THE 1990s: BELIEF SYSTEMS ABOUT THE NATURE OF REALITY

In striving to make sense of the world, researchers seem to work from different beliefs about the nature of reality. Of the various terms used to describe these beliefs I have chosen the terms positivist paradigm and interpretive paradigm. Students need to recognise that my drawing of this distinction and my attempts at using these terms are unlikely to be acceptable to all academics. A research paradigm is a network of coherent ideas about the nature of the world and of the functions of researchers which, adhered to by a group of researchers, conditions the patterns of their thinking and underpins their research actions.

3.1   The positivist research paradigm

To the positivist there is a reality 'out there' in the world that exists whether it is observed or not and irrespective of who observes. This reality can be discovered by people observing with their senses. Discoveries about the reality of human actions can be expressed as factual statements - statements about people, about events, and about relationships between them. To the positivist the entire world is rational, it should make sense and, given sufficient time and effort, it should be possible for it to be understood through patient research. The researcher can then explain the reality s/he has discovered to others, because language is an agreed symbolic system for describing reality.

Positivist researchers do not expect that they themselves are significant variables in their research; thus in testing an hypothesis, they expect other researchers handling similar data to come to the same conclusion that they find. Because of this, positivists' preferred method of writing reports is to avoid personal pronouns. 'I' or 'me' is not considered relevant.
Because things and events are real irrespective of the observer, positivists have little difficulty in giving them descriptive labels. Thus labels like 'deviant', 'truant', 'high achiever' or 'drug addict', provided they are carefully defined, are not seen as problematic and so the possessors of these labels can be counted - the quantity can be measured - and subjected to statistical analysis. This is why the methodology of the positivists is often described as 'quantitative'.

The word 'positivist' is not always recognised by those who work within this paradigm and sometimes is used pejoratively by those engaged in alternative paradigms. In return it is sometimes the case that positivist researchers reject the idea of an interpretive paradigm being a valid basis for research.

To the positivist researcher the purpose of research is to describe and understand the phenomena of the world and to share the findings with others. Understanding enables one to explain how particular events occur and how they are linked in a theoretical structure. It may provide predictions about future events.

3.2 The interpretive research paradigm

The interpretive researcher cannot accept the idea of there being a reality 'out there' which exists irrespective of people, for reality is seen as a construct of the human mind. People perceive and so construe the world in ways which are often *similar* but not necessarily the *same*. So there can be different understandings of what is real. Concepts of reality can vary from one person to another. Instead of reality being 'out there', it is the observers who are 'out there'. They are part of the world which they are observing and so, by observing, may change what they are trying to observe. The interpretive researcher considers that the rationality of one observer may not be the same as the rationality of another, and so accepts that when these two observers talk to each other the world may not seem 'rational' and 'make sense'. The interpretive researcher sees language as a *more-or-less* agreed symbolic system, in which different people may have some differences in their meanings; in consequence the sharing of accounts of what has been observed is always to some extent problematic. Because of differences in perception, in interpretation and in language it is not surprising that people have different views on what is real.

Interpretive researchers reject the positivists' view that the social world can be understood in terms of general statements about human actions. To them the descriptions of human actions are based on social meanings, and people living together interpret the meanings of each other, and these meanings change through social intercourse.

Interpretive researchers recognise that by asking questions or by observing they may change the situation which they are studying. They recognise themselves as potential variables in the enquiry and so, in writing reports, may use personal pronouns.

The data collected by interpretive researchers are usually verbal - fieldwork notes, diaries, and transcripts and reports of conversations. Sometimes interpretive data can be analysed numerically but more usually they are not open to the quantitative statistical analysis used by positivists. They are usually richer, in a language sense, than positivist data and, perhaps because of this quality, the methodology of the interpretive researchers is described as 'qualitative'.

Phenomenology, ethnomethodology, hermeneutics and social anthropology are more or less alternative labels for the interpretive paradigm. Each has its own adherents, who will probably challenge the simplicity of the previous sentence! Ethnography is a branch of this paradigm, concerned with participant observation - where the observer is not 'a fly on the wall', but becomes a participant in the activity which s/he is studying.

To the interpretive researcher the purpose of research is to describe and interpret the phenomena of the world in attempts to get shared meanings with others. Interpretation is a search for deep perspectives on particular events and for theoretical insights. It may offer possibilities, but no certainties, as to the outcome of future events.

* * * * *

Murgatroyd's day

A positivist researcher was collecting data on safety in laboratories. A questionnaire sent to the head of department where Murgatroyd worked elicited this response to a question.

> Please describe any dangerous incidents in your laboratories which have occurred in the previous five weeks using the format set out below by underlining the most appropriate term'
>
> Scale of the incident: <u>minor</u> / major
>
> Number of people involved: one, <u>two</u>, three, more than three
>
> Injuries sustained: <u>none</u>, minor injuries requiring first aid, major injuries entailing doctor

Murgatroyd was a first-year chemistry student. He spent each Thursday morning doing experiments in the laboratory. On one particular Thursday he met a fellow student over lunch after completing his lab work, then he was interviewed by a safety officer, had a tutorial later in the afternoon, went home to his mother's house for tea and in the evening met his girl-friend in the local pub. Each asked the same question, 'What did you do in the lab this morning?' If Murgatroyd had been carrying a tape recorder throughout the afternoon and evening, these are the answers that an interpretive researcher might have extracted from the tape.

To his fellow student.

> Well, we had to do the whole thing twice, that's why I'm late. That twit Bill messed it up again, he didn't read the instructions properly. It wasted so much time when all we wanted to do was to get the thing finished.

To the safety officer.

> Well, we were trying to find out about how a particular compound is formed under rather specialised conditions. It's quite a tricky experiment really and I'm not sure we got it right.

To his tutor.

> We managed to complete the second experiment but the result was not quite as we expected. I think we may have made a mistake in part of the procedure, but the instructions seemed rather ambiguous in places.

To his mother.
> Oh, it was the usual boring chemistry experiment, nothing special about it. When's tea going to be ready?

To his girl-friend.
> It was a really good laugh this morning. Bill nearly blew the place to bits. He put these chemicals in totally the wrong order and if I hadn't pulled the plug out quick we might have ended up as strawberry jam on the walls. You've got to have quick reactions if you're going to be a chemist!

[With acknowledgements to W G Fleming (1986) who invented this story, which I have adapted].

4. THE ETHICS OF SOCIAL RESEARCH

In the conduct of social research I suggest there are three major ethical values: respect for persons; respect for truth; and respect for democratic values. (Cf the *Ethical Guidelines* of the British Educational Research Association, 1992) They can be expressed like this.

The research ethic of respect for persons

> *Researchers, in taking and using data from persons, should do so in ways which recognise those persons' initial ownership of the data and which respect them as fellow human beings who are entitled to dignity and privacy.*

To tape record a conversation without revealing the presence of a tape recorder, or to write a report which reveals the identity of someone who has not given permission for the identity to be revealed, or to quote from a private conversation without permission of the speaker, are actions which must be judged to lack respect for persons - and therefore are unethical for a researcher.

A helpful device used by some researchers when planning and then negotiating participation in research is an ethical statement. This explains to participants the purposes and procedures of the research, describes the arrangements for protecting privacy, indicates who will have access to raw data taken from participants, sets out the arrangements envisaged for publication of findings, and states if and when the archive of the research will be destroyed. Where there is a team of researchers each member of the team signs the ethical statement to indicate acceptance of the ethical procedures defined for the research.

The research ethic of respect for truth

> *Researchers are expected to be truthful in data collection, analysis and the reporting of findings.*

To fabricate data, or to deliberately fudge the analysis or reporting of data in order to produce erroneous conclusions, is reprehensible and unacceptable.
In order to safeguard research from the accusation of untruthfulness, the keeping of systematic and careful records in a project archive is recommended. In principle it should be possible for another researcher to work backwards through the archive from the conclusions of a research report to the raw data and thereby be able to verify the conclusions.

The research ethic of respect for democratic values

> *Researchers in a democratic society can expect certain freedoms, viz: the freedom to investigate and to ask questions, the freedom to give and to receive information, the freedom to express ideas and to criticise the ideas of others, and the freedom to publish research findings. These freedoms are essentially subject to responsibilities imposed by the ethics of respect for persons and respect for truth: provided that these responsibilities are honoured, researchers can expect the freedom to do these things without endangering themselves or their livelihood.*

* * * * *

Inevitably there are problems which these principles raise. Some examples will serve to illustrate this point, but here is not the place to parade the arguments which may help resolve them. Does using data from young children in classrooms require their permission, or their parents, before it can be used in research reports even in anonymised form? Does a fictional rewrite of data, intended either to protect the sources, or to present findings effectively to an audience, violate the second ethic? Does the freedom to investigate and to publish findings entitle a researcher to embarrass the management of a school or college? What are the rights of a research sponsor to restrict the publication of findings by a researcher which could damage the sponsor's enterprise? Ethical issues are not necessarily straightforward!

* * * * *

Chapter One ON THE NATURE OF SOCIAL RESEARCH

It was the university's degree awarding ceremony for the faculty of social science. On the platform sat the academic staff, resplendent in their black and coloured robes. In the tiered rows of the concert hall, hired annually for this ceremony, sat first the new graduates, suited and gowned for the only time in their student careers, and then their proud parents and sweethearts (not more than two tickets per student) stacked to the very roof of the hall. As name after name was announced, the owner climbed onto the platform, shook hands with the very-distinguished-person, occasionally exchanged a few private words - presumably of praise or of enquiry into future career, and received a degree certificate. After every five the audience clapped in a standard routine which, after nearly two hours, had become a simple ritual. Everyone, including the very-distinguished-person, was beginning to look tired. Suddenly a very elegant student was called, her blond hair cascading over the shoulders of a black gown which seemed a Parisian creation, not an off-the-peg job, as she cat-walked across the stage. The very-distinguished-person, like many in the audience, was clearly startled: he swayed slightly on his feet. To steady himself he reached out and grabbed the nearby microphone stand. In consequence their conversation was relayed around the concert hall. 'What are you doing when you leave', asked he. 'Well I was going home, but have you other ideas', she replied.

Without shared meanings there are endless confusions. The purpose of this chapter has been to offer meanings about the nature of social research which, if they can be shared, may reduce confusion.

*   *   *   *   *

It has been said that, while the natural scientists stand on each others shoulders, the social scientists stamp on each others faces. If this is the case, it is perhaps because both the topography and deep structure of the natural sciences are less complicated than that of the social sciences. By and large the natural sciences involve empirical research with theoretical purposes involving searches for generalisations within a positivist paradigm and with fellow researchers as the prime audience. Even the ethics are simpler, being predominantly respect for truth: permission of chemicals is not needed before they are made to react, nor is there usually a problem about reporting on what happened! Contrast that with the varied forms of social science described in this chapter and hence the opportunities for unshared meanings, consequent confusions and internecine warfare! To avoid this it is important that research students in the social sciences, as part of their training, strive for a sympathetic understanding of the overall nature of social science. Whether the present account serves that purpose remains to be seen, but I challenge those fellow academics who disagree with what I have said in this chapter, to write their own account before they stamp on my face!

Chapter Two

ON THE POLITICS OF RESEARCH IN EDUCATION

Sections

1.	HOW IS EDUCATION TO BE DEFINED?	19
2.	EDUCATIONAL RESEARCH AND POLICY MAKING IN EDUCATION	21
3.	ELITISM AND MERITOCRACY THROUGH EDUCATION	23
4.	EDUCATIONAL IDEOLOGIES	25
5.	THE POLITICAL ROLE FOR EDUCATIONAL RESEARCH	28

Chapter Two ON THE POLITICS OF RESEARCH IN EDUCATION

In the previous chapter some of the parameters of research which are potentially applicable to all areas of social research were described. The rest of the book is about only one of these areas: research in education. This chapter starts with the question "How is education to be defined?' and then explores the relationship between the methods of educational research and the methods of educational politics. Although writing for a community of scholars who try to transcend national boundaries, it is perhaps inevitable that much of my material comes from England. Not only is it more familiar to me, but the rapid changes which have happened during the period since 1988, under the political direction of a Conservative government, provide excellent material for exploring the relationship between researcher and politician. During this period the educational systems of the United Kingdom, and that of England in particular, have changed from being the least politically-controlled in the world to perhaps the most!

* * * * *

Prior to the Education Reform Act of 1988 the national government of the United Kingdom had no direct control over the curriculum or pedagogy of schools. An illustration of this is the story from the period of World War II when Britain was fighting for its survival and every one was involved in the war effort. Winston Churchill, Prime Minister, said to R A Butler 'Can't you tell the teachers to make the children in schools more patriotic'. Butler declined, saying: 'As Minister of Education I have no say in what is done in our schools.'

* * * * *

1. HOW IS EDUCATION TO BE DEFINED?

It is valuable for everyone who is engaging in educational research from time to time to write down what they mean by 'education'. Unlike the definition offered in the previous chapter for 'research' this one is more difficult. In the 1960s and 1970s there was much debate about what education means; today the concept of 'education' seems to be strangely located within the positivist paradigm, as though we all give it the same meaning. Yet this is clearly not the case. Some see it as acquiring useful knowledge and skills, some as developing personally and socially, some about how to earn a living in the future, and others about how to increase the gross national product in the future.

With some trepidation, I set out my present beliefs on the nature of education. This is done in the spirit of offering it for criticism and of searching for new insights, but also as a basis for ideas which I shall develop later in the book. It draws heavily on the writing of M V C

Jeffreys in a book entitled *Glaucon: an Enquiry into the Aims of Education* (1950), but also includes the concept of the 'worthwhile' used by R S Peters in *Ethics and Education* (1966).

Education is:

first, the experience and nurture of personal and social development towards worthwhile living; and

secondly, the acquisition, development, transmission, conservation, and renewal of worthwhile culture.

This is only a framework definition, and as such is one that probably many people can share. It embraces the activities of, for example, learners (experience, acquisition, development), of teachers (nurture, development, transmission), of scholars and librarians (conservation), and of artists, scientists, engineers, politicians, and researchers (development, renewal).

The crunch comes when we try to define 'worthwhile living' and 'worthwhile culture'. It is here that the arguments begin, for there are many different views of what is worthwhile living and worthwhile culture. For example, the introduction of the national curriculum in England and Wales was a massive attempt by government to define what shall be transmitted to children in schools as worthwhile culture, while the hidden curriculum of elitism and competition introduces some aspects of what the British Conservative government (at the time of writing) sees as worthwhile living.

To illustrate the power and complexity of the definition let me expose my own position on what constitutes 'worthwhile living' - which is very different from the one based on elitism mentioned above. It is expressed in the idea of conviviality, which I have developed from Ivan Illich's (1973) *Tools for Conviviality* and E F Schumacher's (1973) *Small is Beautiful*.

> Conviviality has a profound meaning concerned with the nature of human life. A convivial person is trying to achieve a state of deep and satisfying harmony with the world, which gives joyful meaning to life. Convivial people are striving for harmony with their environment, with their fellows, and with their self.

> Striving for harmony with their *physical environment* convivial people use it for their needs, but do not exploit it; they conserve the land and the living things which the land supports and, seeing themselves as stewards, aim to safeguard the land for future generations.

> Striving for harmony with their *intellectual environment* convivial people seek to explore and to understand the world of ideas and, where appropriate, to relate them purposefully to the world of action.
>
> Striving for harmony with their *fellows*, they seek to co-operate rather than to compete with them; they neither exploit them nor are exploited by them; they try to live in concord with their fellows - to love and be loved.
>
> Striving for harmony with *the self*, convivial people have sufficient understanding of both their rationality and their emotions to develop their talents effectively; by using their talents harmoniously in relation to society and the environment they become self-reliant and thus experience the joy of convivial life.

I have met people who share this belief and others who have strong opposition to parts of it. This brings me bluntly to the point that the edifices of education, and therefore of educational research, inevitably stand on the bed rock of ideology. Our educational thoughts and actions are consequences of our beliefs about human nature, about equality, about freedom, and about the purposes of life. Individuals rarely stand alone in holding to beliefs, but tend to subscribe to the ideological stance of whatever societal grouping they belong to.

2. EDUCATIONAL RESEARCH AND POLICY MAKING IN EDUCATION

Educational researchers share the aim of seeking to advance knowledge about education through systematic enquiry and critical debate. As discussed in the previous chapter, in common with other social researchers, most (perhaps all) of us see ourselves as governed by three ethical principles: respect for persons (ie people should not be abused); respect for truth (ie falsehood is unacceptable); and respect for democratic values (ie research should be open). The research concept of 'critical debate' is fundamental. It entails opening one's work to the scrutiny of others in order first to search for errors and fallacies, and secondly to seek creative insights into its future development. This is always problematic because deep down our human nature wants to hide mistakes, while our research ethic insists that they be exposed.

Educational researchers seem to expect that educational policy makers will also base their decisions on open discussion of research evidence. Until defeated by cynicism, they expect policy makers to subscribe to the same ethics and to the same procedures that they use. Researchers expect policy makers to use evidence, not hearsay, and to consult teachers and weigh arguments, not issue fiats.

Here lies the problem for politicians. Politicians have insufficient time (they may have only a short period in office) to become expert on issues. They cannot expose their intentions to critical scrutiny because the admission of errors or fallacies would be seen as political weakness rather than intellectual integrity. They cannot forget the ballot box, for their every action may affect votes at the next election. In consequence the procedures of politicians are quite different from those of researchers. The slogan and sound bite are more important than the reasoned argument. Belligerent confrontation is better than intellectual challenge. And many also carry the hidden agenda of personal ambition, which needs quick success and experience of many offices of state.

Education in Britain since 1988 has become a political battlefield. The ruling politicians dismiss many of the views of what they call the 'education establishment' as being out-of-touch with the modern world of competition and market-forces. For example, at the time of writing:

* Raw examination results of schools and local authorities are published in the newspapers as league tables, irrespective of expert opinion that these are misleading.
* Public examinations at 16 and 18 (GCSE and A-level) are not to have more than 20% of marks coming from coursework, irrespective of expert opinion that high proportions of coursework (as introduced in recent years) have enhanced the quality of learning.
* The powers of local education authorities have been steadily reduced at a time when expert opinion recognises that many of them have made major contributions to the improvement of school practice in recent years through central services, inservice training programmes and inspection.
* Teacher training has been edged away from the universities and colleges towards school-based training, contrary to most expert opinion that this will be an ineffective way of providing training.

These decisions by policy makers are not the result of analysis of all the available evidence and consultation of expert opinion. There is no underpinning empirical research which has been publicly discussed. Relevant knowledge and experience are not only ignored, but derided. There is no critical debate between policy makers and expert opinion. There is only decision by politicians in a hurry.

The present British government, and their advisers, have treated educational researchers, among other educational professionals, to what Stephen Ball (1990) calls a discourse of derision. He says in *Politics and Policy Making in Education*:

'This discourse of derision acted to debunk and displace not only specific words and meanings - progressivism and comprehensivism, for example - but also the speakers of these words, those 'experts', 'specialists' and 'professionals' referred to as the 'educational establishment'. These privileged speakers have been displaced, their control over meaning lost, their professional preferences replaced by ... parental choice, the market, efficiency and management. A new discursive regime has been established and with it new forms of authority.' (p18)

It has been constantly reiterated that standards are falling, that too many teachers are either weak or subversive, that important subjects in schools are neglected, that teacher education is failing, and that the LEAs are conniving in this deterioration. These utterances, coming from a variety of right-wing think-tanks and regularly headlined in certain newspapers, have been in the main unsubstantiated assertion and argument-by-selected-instance. The question of what counts as significant evidence has been ignored. As Ball says:

'The role of expert knowledge and research is regarded as less dependable than political intuition and common sense accounts of what people want." (p32)

This discourse of derision has served to prepare the ground for ideological change.

Ball stresses that the ideological change which our education system and schools are experiencing is not simple. He refers to

'the messy realities of influence, pressure, dogma, expediency, conflict, compromise, intransigence, resistance, error, opposition and pragmatism in the policy process." (p9)

3. ELITISM AND MERITOCRACY THROUGH EDUCATION

Ball describes the present discourse of educational change as one of 'elite-pluralism' and he illustrates the conflict in these words:

'Old conservative interests are at odds with new, manufacturing capital with finance capital, the Treasury with the DTI, the neo-liberals with the neo-conservatives, wets with drys, Elizabeth House with Number 10, the DES with itself, Conservative Central Office with the Shires.' (p19)

Ball is one of the few researchers in the realm of empirical research (he interviewed 49 educational administrators and politicians) who have tried to understand contemporary change in education. Another is Stewart Ranson who, in the early 1980s reported on an interview with an anonymous DES civil servant who had said:

'We are beginning to create aspirations which society cannot match ... When young people drop off the education production line and cannot find work at all, or [cannot find] work which meets their abilities and expectations, then we are only creating frustration with perhaps disturbing social consequences. We have to select: to ration the educational opportunities so that society can cope with the output of

> education. ... If we have a highly educated and idle population we may possibly anticipate more serious conflict. People must be educated once more to know their place." (p241)

Brian Simon, in his widely read book *Does Education Matter* (1985), from which I draw the quotation, has made strong use of this sinister perspective.

I would like to relate that statement to a book written much earlier, in 1958, by Michael Young called *The Rise of the Meritocracy* which purports to be an essay written in 2034 about the crisis in education!

Young saw more clearly than anybody at that time, the way that education was going. He saw the creeping trend towards a two-class system based on intellectual merit, with an upper class - a meritocracy - enjoying privilege and power as a consequence of their trained intelligence, and a lower class, of inferior intelligence, educated for the menial tasks of society. Young was wrong about the form of government intervention which produced the meritocracy, for he predicted that grammar school teachers would be paid similar salaries to industrial scientists as a result of legislation! He didn't see that market forces would be used as the engine of change. But he was right in predicting that education would be used to create a meritocratic elite and that egalitarian approaches to education would wane.

> It did not matter so much about the defective, maladjusted and delinquent ... It did not matter so much about the secondary modern schools. In an ideal world, not hampered by shortage of resources, the unfortunate could have large sums spent on them too. But it was not, has not been, nor ever will be, an ideal world. The choice was between priorities, and there was no doubt how the decision had to go. What mattered most were primary schools, where the pupils were being divided into the gifted and the ungifted; and, above all, the grammar schools where the gifted received their due. They had to have more generous endowments. And they got them. (p48)

It is interesting to rewrite that in the language of today, remembering that Young's fable purports to be a historical account written in 2034.

> It did not matter so much about special needs children. It did not matter so much about the local authority secondary schools. The choice was between priorities. What mattered most were the primary schools, where the children were being divided into the gifted and the ungifted by national curriculum assessment; and, above all, the grant-maintained schools and city technology colleges where the gifted would receive their due. They had to have more generous endowments. And they got them.

There was a time when many of us felt that politics should be kept out of education: we now know that that is not possible. In particular, as researchers, we need to understand that policy conclusions which we may draw from painstaking researches, can be irrelevant to those politicians who do not share our fundamental beliefs.

I suggest that the really significant divide in politics is over the share-out of resources. Gandhi said that there is sufficient in the world for each person's need, there is insufficient for each one's greed. The major divide in political thinking is about where the boundary lies between need and greed, and about what mechanisms should serve to distribute resources in relation to need and greed.

The left look for an equitable distribution on moral grounds; they argue for centralised planning to achieve this, otherwise the aspiration of some individuals overrides the need of others. The right believe that a disproportionate distribution is necessary on pragmatic grounds of efficiency and the need for progress; they argue for market forces to achieve this, thus fostering the aspiration of some individuals to create an elite. The left see the unbridled working of market forces as immoral; the right see centralised planning as humanly impractical.

How does this affect education? Those who subscribe to the ideology of the left see education in part as a means of learning to share resources. Those who subscribe to the ideology of the right, see education in part as a means of learning to compete successfully for resources. Thus the left seeks a child-centred education in which cooperation is valued and the right seeks a knowledge-and-skills education in which competition is valued.

* * * * *

If a teacher asks a child to share ten sweets between five children the correct answer for the left is 'two sweets each', while the correct answer for the right is 'four have one sweet each and the fifth child has six'. I don't believe that this is a particularly naive analysis; naivety is when we forget that ideology underpins our thinking about what is correct.

* * * * *

4. EDUCATIONAL IDEOLOGIES

In the period between say 1950 and 1980 two educational ideologies were in evidence in British schools: their followers became known as the 'traditionalists' and the 'progressives'. The traditionalists were associated with separation of children at 11 into different schools (grammar, technical and modern), classes streamed according to ability, didactic teaching methods, sitting in rows, competitive games, classical literature, etc. while the progressives were associated with comprehensive schools, mixed ability classes, discovery teaching methods, sitting in groups, collaborative games, popular literature, etc. Sadly these differences in professional opinion about the most effective forms of schooling were not illuminated by much research, and such research as was carried out tended to be positivist and so to miss out the essential detail which interpretative research might have provided. During the period there were both Labour and Conservative governments in power. Since government was rigorously excluded from considerations of curriculum and pedagogy in schools the major political outcome of the struggle between the two ideologies was a structural one - the slow ending of selection at 11 and the development of comprehensive schools.

By the 1990s it became apparent that the ideological dichotomy was being replaced by something more complex. The following account sees four distinct ideologies and, in my view, helps to explain what is happening today in relation to government and educational research. Although inevitably simplistic it is, I submit, the case that most education policy-makers and educationists, other than those who are totally pragmatic, today act and talk in ways which locate them in, or at least near to, one of four groups, even if they would deny the allegiance. Three of these groups were identified by Stephen Ball (1990) in *Politics and Policy Making in Education*, the other group (the 'competitive elitists') I described in a booklet called *The Great Education Conspiracy?* (1992), although without using that name.

The *cultural restorationists* define education in terms of the transmission of traditional culture by authoritative teachers. For them teaching needs to develop conceptions of English, mathematics, science, geography, history, art, literature and music which are valued in an elitist tradition and defined in a national curriculum. National heritage is significant. The acquisition of worthwhile knowledge is more important than engaging in creative or critical processes. There should be formal relationships between teachers and learners. Summative assessment by examination and selection by academic ability should lead to separate schooling arrangements. Competitiveness is to be encouraged. Scholarship is more important than empirical educational research.

The *industrial trainers* define education in terms of future adult work in a society where economic growth must be a paramount concern. For them teaching needs to promote habits of punctuality, self-discipline, obedience and trained effort, and needs to provide appropriate skills and knowledge which will contribute to the creation of industrial wealth. Inspection reports should facilitate the operation of market forces in schools which will foster excellence. Sensible innovation is valued. There is a shift of emphasis from teaching to learning; formative assessment and graded assessment systems are valued. Co-operation among pupils, and competition between teams, is to be encouraged. Industrial management styles should be developed in schools and colleges and educational research should support such change.

Chapter Two ON THE POLITICS OF RESEARCH IN EDUCATION

The *competitive elitists* see education as a means of restructuring society into a small elite and a large underclass. The elite can be selected by the education system and then must be given an education suitable for their future role as managers, scientists and technologists. The underclass need an education which will: (a) train those who get jobs with the skills needed for the job; (b) inculcate a moral code which protects the interests of the elite; and (c) develop a compliant and unquestioning attitude which accepts their place in society. Competition is not only the way of developing the elite, it is the way of enabling the underclass to accept their inferior status. It follows that summative assessment by formal tests and examinations is important as is the formal inspection of schools. Reflection and research are potentially dangerous activities because they may challenge the fundamental premise of this stance.

The *rational progressives* (Ball calls them 'new progressives') define education in terms of development of the learner's personal potential. They look for innovation in curriculum, pedagogy, and assessment which is justified by research evidence and logical argument. The emphasis is learner-centred, constructivist, democratic, and collaborative. Motivation is very important and there is a strong orientation towards individual performance and graded assessments. Formative assessment is important. There is a strong interest in educational processes which focus on skills, applications and problem solving. The rational progressives hold to the concepts of the reflective practitioner, of action research, and of challenge and support inspection, as means of improving practice.

It is important to note that for the rational progressives, every professional judgement and educational decision must be underpinned by justifiable theory, or by a rationale deriving from evidence or logical argument. Unlike the former group of progressives (whom I am inclined to call the 'fashion progressives'), they are unimpressed by judgements and decisions which 'follow the crowd'. They want to know why something is appropriate in a particular situation.

* * * * *

In the early 1970s I worked with student teachers in primary schools in two neighbouring local education authorities in the East Midlands of England who were both considered, by themselves and by others, to be 'progressive'. In one, children had to use pointed scissors and not rounded scissors, and could use clay but not plasticene. In the other, children had to use rounded scissors and could work with plasticene. In many of the classrooms of one, a rotating pattern of groupwork prevailed, in the other classwork prevailed. I never obtained an explanation for these differences other than , 'Well that's the way we do it in this authority's schools'. Local fashion was the justification; the rational justifications had been forgotten. The idea that some approaches were more suited to some classrooms than others was ignored.

* * * * *

Perhaps at this stage you are saying: if decisions about education are so firmly influenced by the ideology of people in power what hope is there for researchers who are of a different political persuasion? The answer is that there has perhaps never been a time when it is so important to use the systematic and critical processes of research to tease out the truth. The truth which we need to explore lies not only in the outcomes of actions but in the minds of the actors. More needs to be known about the beliefs of those who wield power and who plan for the future. Ideologies need to be made overt and subjected to public scrutiny so that they can be debated, criticised, and developed.

Pajares (1992) has made a detailed study of beliefs and educational research. He writes that 'defining beliefs is at best a game of player's choice.' He adds:

> They travel in disguise and often under alias - attitudes, values, judgements, axioms, opinions, ideology, perceptions, conceptions, conceptual systems, preconceptions, dispositions, implicit theories, explicit theories, personal theories, internal mental processes, action strategies, rules of practice, practical principles, perspectives, repertories of understanding, and social strategy, to name but a few that can be found in the literature. (p309)

He gives a well-documented list of 16 reasonable assumptions about beliefs, including these:

> Beliefs are formed early and tend to self-perpetuate, persevering even against contradictions caused by reason, time, schooling, or experience. (p324)
>
> The belief system has an adaptive function in helping individuals define and understand the world and themselves. (p325)
>
> Beliefs are instrumental in defining tasks and selecting the cognitive tools with which to interpret, plan, and make decisions regarding such tasks; hence, they play a critical role in defining behaviour and organising knowledge and information. (p325)

His conclusion is that:

> When they are clearly conceptualised, when their key assumptions are examined, when precise meanings are consistently understood and adhered to, and when specific belief constructs are properly assessed and investigated, beliefs can be ... the single most important construct in educational research. (p329)

5. THE POLITICAL ROLE OF EDUCATIONAL RESEARCH

Social research has a vital role in supporting democracy - in finding out what is happening in society, reflecting on it, evaluating it, thinking creatively about it, and communicating the findings to as wide an audience as possible in order that the future can be determined by the democratic will of the people and not by the autocratic will of an elite. Insofar as learning is a central activity of human beings, educational research should be at the centre of social research.

Education today in the United Kingdom is going through a maelstrom of change. A national curriculum for ages 5 to 16 has been introduced couched mainly in terms of a transmission theory of learning. Extensive summative testing of children at 7, 11, and 14 has been introduced with some results being published in league tables to help parents select schools for their children to attend. Schools, colleges and universities are being put on a business footing, with an ethos of competition. Coursework assessment has been reduced and replaced by more examination assessment. The regular appraisal of teachers has being introduced and in the future could be used as a basis for a merit-pay system. Teacher training is being changed from being predominantly higher education-based to more school-based. The local education authorities are losing most of their powers. The sizes of classes are rising. Inspection of schools has become four-yearly, rigid, comprehensive, very challenging and non-supportive. Few of these changes are based on research evidence. These government-induced changes are being wrought in a society where massive unintended changes are happening - increasing unemployment, increasing crime, decline in manufacturing industry, and change in family life, to name but a few. At such a time researchers have an urgent responsibility to locate their researches in significant issues, and to organise their work for maximum impact.

These research issues are reactive ones, meaning that changes have happened and there is a need for researchers to react - to monitor change, analyse, evaluate, reflect, and report on it. But beyond these there are issues where educational researchers should be proactive. For example, Stewart Ranson (1992) has argued that educational researchers should broaden their typical preoccupation with schools, teachers, children and classrooms, to embrace the education of all members of society. He says:

> This understanding can place education at the centre of the issues of our time. The processes and conditions of learning in the workplace, in the home and in the community become as important as those within the classroom or lecture hall. Understanding the processes of learning, moreover, can inform knowledge of creativity in the arts, discovery in the sciences and innovation in the world of practice. Thus the intellectual challenge for research and teaching ... is to focus upon developing analysis of, and enabling the conditions for, learning throughout society.

At the same time we need to create a political situation where research evidence and expert opinion are wanted, welcomed and debated, so that when decisions about the future of our society are made, reason and not rhetoric is triumphant. These points are developed further in Chapter Nine.

* * * * *

At the time of writing this section, Hammersley and Scarth wrote a scathing critique (1993) of a Department for Education discussion document entitled *'Curriculum organisation and practice in primary schools'* which was written by Alexander, Rose and Woodhead (1992) (and popularly known as the *'Report of the three wise men'*).

Hammersley and Scarth begin their paper with this paragraph:

> The proper function of educational research is widely regarded as being to inform policy-makers and practitioners, and thereby to improve education. At the same time, there has long been concern about the lack of impact of research on policy and practice. Sometimes policy-makers and practitioners are blamed for taking insufficient account of research findings. Alternatively research is criticised for being insufficiently relevant to the work of those whom it is intended to inform. But behind this conception of the role of research, and the complaints about its failure to fulfil this role effectively, there often seems to be an assumption that the influence of research on practice will necessarily be benign, so that it is in everyone's interests to maximise that influence. ... relatively little attention has been paid to the misinterpretation and misuse of research findings. In this paper we examine a recent example ... (p489)

After five pages of carefully documented argument, Hammersley and Scarth conclude:

> First, it employs misleadingly selective interpretation of evidence ... Second, it engages in over-interpretation of the evidence to support a particular view: claims are made which the evidence cited simply cannot support. (p496)

It is however their third argument that is of particular significance to this chapter.

> The third ground for complaint concerns the relationship between the findings of research and educational practice that the report assumes, and the consequent relationship between educationists and teachers that it implies. In what they say, the authors presume that the findings of research provide a strong basis for not just identifying problems but for recommending solutions. In our view, even were educational research to be much more highly developed than it currently is, having solved the serious methodological problems that currently bedevil it, there is little chance that it would be capable of playing the sort of directive role which the authors assume. This arises, in large part, from the character of educational practice. It does not consist of the implementation of policies, but rather of attempts to realise multiple values by means of judgements about situations, judgements that may be informed by research but will be shaped more by the sedimented experience of the practitioner and her or his local knowledge. (p496)

Chapter Two ON THE POLITICS OF RESEARCH IN EDUCATION

Hammersley and Scarth then express their concern at current government interventions in relation to their view of the proper role of research.

> ... what must be done, above all, is to create a context in which the development and exercise of the professional expertise of teachers is facilitated. Yet the interventions of which this report is a part are calculated to do quite the opposite ... These interventions seem to represent a concerted policy to establish and operate central control over education, and it is in the promotion of this goal that the findings of educational research have been misused in this report. (p496)

*   *   *   *   *

This establishes a convenient link with the next chapter, which asks the question 'what is educational research?'

Chapter Three

ON THE KINDS OF RESEARCH IN EDUCATIONAL SETTINGS

Sections

1.	UNCERTAINTIES ABOUT RESEARCH IN EDUCATIONAL SETTINGS	33
2.	A DEFINITION OF EDUCATIONAL RESEARCH	38
3.	A DEFINITION OF SOCIOLOGICAL RESEARCH IN EDUCATION	42
4.	A DEFINITION OF PSYCHOLOGICAL RESEARCH IN EDUCATION	44
5.	OTHER DISCIPLINARY RESEARCHES IN EDUCATION	45
6.	EDUCATIONAL ACTION RESEARCH	46
7.	DISCUSSION	51

Chapter Three ON THE KINDS OF RESEARCH IN EDUCATIONAL SETTINGS

Two long-haired, bearded, polo-necked men holding wine glasses, talking together at a party featured in a cartoon in the Times Educational Supplement several years ago. Presumably in answer to a question, one is saying:

> *Me? Oh well I sort of dabble with a bit of everything in a sense you know whatever's going as it were. Psychology, sociology, economics you name it our boys'll have a crack. No job too big, as they say old man. At a push you could kind of almost say I'm kind of in er educational er research really. (Williams 1976)*

For too long there has been something rather uncertain about educational research, which leaves it wide open to ill-informed criticism and academic snideness. A significant weakness is that there is no generally accepted definition of what it is. Some see it as research that focuses on educational processes; some as research that seeks to improve educational practice; others as any research carried out in educational settings. In this chapter I explore these uncertainties and then suggest that there are several forms of research in educational settings, which merit clear delineation and mutual respect.

1. UNCERTAINTIES ABOUT RESEARCH IN EDUCATIONAL SETTINGS

Educational research rarely attracts public interest, but in December 1993 it was the subject of debate in the UK House of Lords because of the Government's intention, through the 1993 Education Bill, to make the proposed Teacher Training Agency responsible for the funding of some (or all?) educational research instead of the Higher Education Funding Councils.

Speaking in the debate Lord Skidelsky said:

> It is alleged by many noble Lords that the Bill will stifle objective research into education, destroy a healthy research community, or destroy a sound research base, as though all those things already exist and something healthy is being cut down by the Government. Where have noble Lords been living over the past few years? Much of that is simply fantasy. I have had occasion to study professionally much of the research that has taken place and I have also had experience in my own university. Many of the fruits of that research I would describe as an uncontrolled growth of theory, an excessive emphasis on what is called the context in which teaching takes place, which is code for class, gender and ethnic issues, and an extreme paucity of testable hypotheses about what works and does not work.

Earlier in the same speech he said:

> Pedagogy is not analogous to medicine, law or accountancy. There is no theoretically based good practice which defines professional teaching. There are a number of arguments and approaches and they are in contention. ... I can think of few things more destructive of effective teaching than a full

understanding of educational theory. Educational theory is not in that state of development. We can still read with great profit Rousseau's *Emile*, written in the 18th century. We cannot read with great profit a medical text written in the 18th century. That is the difference. Education is an immature discipline and, because of the very strong element of politics, ideology and connection with wider social aims that are always part of the theory of how to teach, that will remain the case and educational theory will always be highly disputable. [Hansard 7 December 1993 col 882-883]

I wrote a fairly vitriolic article in the Times Educational Supplement on this (21 January 1994). I said:

> I have to challenge Lord Skidelsky since he claims authority by saying that he has 'had occasion to study professionally much of the research that has taken place.' Since there are over 200 journals currently reporting on different aspects of educational research, and at least 50 books a year published on research findings, he has been busy. It is regrettable that his comment on these writings is not marked with the scholarship for which he is respected in his own field. Let me illustrate this by responding to a few points made in his speech.

> First let us examine his assertion that 'there is no theoretically based good practice which defines professional teaching.' Much of the good professional practice of teachers, as of doctors and lawyers, is embedded in their experience, and its quality depends upon factors such as their commitment, their enthusiasm, their memory of previous cases and their reflective intelligence. If Lord Skidelsky had read Schon's 'The Reflective Practitioner' he would know this. But underpinning this good professional practice are theoretical ideas. As an example take the following summary account of the constructivist theory of learning:
>
>> Learning has here been defined as the extension, elaboration or modification of children's schemata. Children achieve this by making sense of new knowledge in the light of their existing knowledge. The construction of this sense making is a continual intellectual process, an essential input to which is social interaction. Talk aids the organisation of experience into thought, and is thus central to learning.
>
> This was written by Neville Bennett, Professor of Primary Education at the University of Exeter in a booklet called 'Managing Learning in the Primary Classroom' (1992). I fail to understand how Lord Skidelsky could think, for example, that a full understanding of constructivist theory would be destructive of effective teaching.

> Secondly consider his assertion about ancient texts. I agree that the writings of Rousseau are of profit to teachers, but only in the same way that the writings of Hippocrates are of profit to doctors and of Locke to lawyers. They stimulate thought on philosophical issues, not on effective ways of tackling practical problems.

Thirdly he refers to 'an excessive emphasis on what is called the context in which teaching takes place' coupled with 'an extreme paucity of testable hypotheses about what works and does not work'. Here he shows a glimmer of understanding of one of the great achievements of educational research in recent years, but makes nonsense of it by failing to grasp its significance. The outcomes of teaching depend upon so many variables (in other words contexts are so complicated) that attempts to formulate testable hypotheses about effective teaching are rarely worthwhile. This is why qualitative work within an interpretive paradigm is favoured by many educational researchers in their attempts to advance knowledge and wisdom about classroom practice and management procedure. By contrast, when the concern is to provide knowledge for policy makers, it is quantitative work in a positivist paradigm that is often appropriate.

Finally it seems from his speech that in order to prevent what he sees as 'an uncontrolled growth of theory' he would like to see a quango of eight - whose main concern would be the funding of teacher training - having responsibility for ensuring that better research is carried out. Help!

The academic research community is not complacent. There is much critical debate about the quality, credibility and impact of educational research. There is great awareness of past short-comings and of future potential. There is much concern about how researchers are trained - and how they can construct careers in research. There is disquiet that policy issues such as class size have not been adequately addressed.

But deeper than these there is grave concern about the future of our society. Any society only remains democratic while there is a free flow of information. Research provides one form of information and should entail trained intelligence focusing in depth on significant issues. Now, a society where quangos of government-appointees determine what significant issues are to be researched will soon decline. The uncomfortable issues, the ones that challenge orthodoxy, the ones that question fundamentals, will not gain funding and so this stimulus to the redevelopment of society will be lost. Decline will be inevitable. Please think again, Lord Skidelsky.

Lord Skidelsky replied a week later and while not accepting much of my argument, agreed that educational research should stay with the universities.

The importance of his speech is that it is not just the opinion of one outspoken peer, but is more or less typical of the view of a substantial number of his fellow academics and senior politicians. They fail to see that the reason why there is 'an extreme paucity of testable hypotheses about what works and does not work' is a natural consequence of educational research being predominantly a science of the singular. (Helen Simons used this phrase in a book title in 1980). They judge educational research as though it were a science of the general.

This is an issue which is explored in Chapters Six and Seven. In this chapter this exchange of views serves to open the question, 'What kinds of research are there in educational settings?' In my view it is essential to recognise the plurality of this question. Most writers on educational research seem not to recognise this plurality and so, in espousing their own view as the unique one, endanger it from attacks by those who hold alternative views.

* * * * *

In 1968 Butcher introduced the series of books entitled *Educational Research in Britain*, of which he was editor, by stating that

> 'educational research' covers a multitude of activities. It is interpreted here as empirical research, based on experiment, on social surveys and on the clinical study of individuals'. (p 13)

This definition identifies the field of enquiry as empirical, but gives the enquiry no intention or purpose. It is noteworthy for its reference, at that time, to the study of individuals.

In a reaction against the assumption 'that educational research is a branch of psychology or social science', Peters and White (1969) suggested that

> educational research is sustained systematic enquiry designed to provide us with new knowledge which is relevant to initiating people into desirable states of mind involving depth and breadth of understanding.)

This broadens Butcher's definition to include philosophical and historical study, and gives the purpose of 'initiating people into desirable states of mind'.

Williams (1969), writing in Blond's Encyclopaedia of Education, gave a definition of educational research as:

> the process whereby information relevant to the decisions involved in the improvement of educational practices is obtained. (p235)

In 1973 Nisbet and Entwistle (who three years earlier had published *Educational Research Methods*, which became a standard textbook for students of educational research) gave a definition which included the concept of efficiency, viz:

> Educational research consists in careful, systematic attempts to understand the educational process and, through understanding, to improve its efficiency.

Simon (1978), in his presidential address to the British Educational Research Association in 1977, expressed the view that:

Chapter Three ON THE KINDS OF RESEARCH IN EDUCATIONAL SETTINGS

the focus of educational research must be education, and that its overall function is to assist teachers, administrators, indeed all concerned in the field, to improve the quality of the educational process - and, in so doing, enhance the quality of life. (p5)

These quotations might give the impression that educational research had become free standing and quite distinctive from psychological, sociological, philosophical and historical research, but this was not so. When the Economic and Social Research Council produced its *Postgraduate Training Guidelines* (1991), the chosen description of educational research was a compromise between research on educational processes and research in educational settings.

> Educational research may include any disciplined enquiry which serves educational judgements and decisions or which is conducted in educational settings such as nursery, primary, secondary, further, higher, continuing and adult education; industrial, commercial and professional training; and local and national systems of education. This disciplined enquiry may draw on the methodologies of other social science disciplines, such as sociology, psychology, philosophy, or economics; or its methods and techniques may originate from an eclectic view of how knowledge is best generated and utilised by educational policy makers, educational managers and classroom practitioners.
> *ESRC Postgraduate Training Guidelines* (1991) (p23)

[It is interesting that only the Education panel and two others of the 20 subjects reported on in the *Guidelines* chose to give a description of the nature of research in their subject. Perhaps this is a measure of the uncertainty of educational researchers, or is it the arrogance of the other subject researchers that they consider that the boundaries of their subjects need no definition?]

There is something paternalistic about the phrase 'may draw on the methodologies of other social science disciplines'. However my antagonism to this definition is more fundamental. In my view research in educational settings is only <u>educational research</u> if it is concerned with attempts to improve educational judgements and decisions. Research in educational settings which aims to develop sociological theory, psychological theory, philosophical constructs or historical ideas is not educational research, but <u>sociological, psychological, philosophical or historical research in educational settings</u>.

It is time for educational research to assert that it has come of age. It is time to leave the parental home (if sociology and psychology were the parents) and stand firmly on our own ground. That ground is the educational process of the making of decisions and judgements by practitioners and policy-makers, from the standpoint of trying to improve them.

This argument is not new. In 1977 Brian Simon, in the presidential address to BERA cited above, went onto say:

> Brief raids into educational territory are considered to be a good means of training the specialist sociologist, or psychologist, even if schools used for data collection are left in disarray. Research of this kind is not, in my book, *educational* research. It is psychological or sociological research conducted with educational materials which may, or may not, constitute a significant contribution to education. (Simon 1978, p4)

2. A DEFINITION OF EDUCATIONAL RESEARCH

In 1975, in *An Introduction to Curriculum Research and Development*, Stenhouse wrote:

> A research tradition which is accessible to teachers and which feeds teaching must be created if education is to be significantly improved. (p165)

This often repeated quotation, the ideas associated with it, and the endeavours of the many people which they have inspired, have helped change the climate of teacher opinion about educational research. Once denigrated by teachers as either stating the obvious or incomprehensible, it is now seen by many of them as potentially important for the advancement of educational practice. [It is still, regrettably, denigrated by some right-wing politicians, as discussed earlier].

Nearly 20 years later, David Tripp, in *Critical Incidents in Teaching* (1993) demonstrates through the medium of 62 researched 'critical incidents' the power of critical analysis of everyday occurrences in classrooms. He sees the study of critical incidents as leading to improved professional judgement, and identifies four kinds of judgement as necessary in professional teaching. These are:

1. Practical judgement, which is the basis of every action taken in the conduct of teaching, and the majority of which is made instantly.
2. Diagnostic judgement, which involves using profession-specific knowledge and academic expertise to recognise, describe, understand and explain, and interpret practical judgements.
3. Reflective judgement, which concerns more personal and moral judgements involving the identification, description, exploration and justification of the judgements made and values implicit and espoused in practical (teaching) decisions and their explanations.
4. Critical judgement, which, through formal investigation, involves challenge to and evaluation of the judgements and values revealed by reflection. (p140)

Chapter Three ON THE KINDS OF RESEARCH IN EDUCATIONAL SETTINGS

Tripp is in no doubt that if educational research seeks to improve practice it needs to be grounded in educational events and not in academic theories. He says:

> It was only when I recognised the fact that I had been very successful in the classroom when I was very ignorant of what academics considered knowledge essential to teaching, that I became aware of the difference between the knowledge of academics and the knowledge of teachers. It has since become clear that most academic educational knowledge is of very little use to teachers and that teachers' knowledge and understanding of their practice is seriously under-represented and discounted in the university discipline of education. ...
>
> ... It appears to me that the most promising means of improving teaching is by grounding educational research (and thus theory) in the realities of teachers' everyday experience. Overall, I believe that an approach based on the interpretation of critical incidents has the potential to change the nature of the teaching profession by dealing with the fundamental practical, political and epistemological problems of education in teachers' terms (p152)

* * * * *

Trying to synthesise the above ideas in the form of a definition, leads to this. I believe that a definition like this needs to be nailed to the door and printed on the letterhead of everyone who claims to be an educational researcher!

Educational research aims critically to inform educational judgements and decisions in order to improve educational action.

The reason for referring to 'judgements' and 'decisions' is this. Educational action depends upon judgements as to what is worthwhile and decisions as to what to do. As such it embraces both practice and policy. For example, looking at my personal definition of education given in the previous chapter, the provision of experience, nurture, acquisition, development, transmission, conservation, and renewal, all entail people making <u>decisions</u>, and the idea that these should contribute to worthwhile living and worthwhile culture, entail people making <u>judgements</u> about what is worthwhile.

There are many ways of working towards the end of critically informing educational judgements and decisions in order to improve educational action. This definition embraces the realms of empirical, reflective and creative research; the categories of theoretical, evaluative and action research; the search for generalisations and the study of singularities; the audiences of researchers, practitioners and policy-makers; and the positivist and interpretive paradigms.

Some examples help to illustrate the argument. All of the following quotations are of abstracts, written by the authors. Some of these authors originally trained as sociologists, some as psychologists and some in other disciplines. But in the following papers they were, in my judgement, predominantly acting as educationists.

> **Some sink, some float: National Curriculum assessment and accountability** Abbott D, Broadfoot P, Croll P, Osborn M, and Pollard A (1994) *British Educational Research Journal* 20(2) 155-174
>
> This article considers the Government's stated aims of introducing to British primary schools an assessment process which would be simultaneously criterion-referenced, formative, moderated, related to progression, and evaluative. Accountability, which has provided the main rationale for the process, presupposes reliability. In 1991, as part of the Bristol Primary Assessment, Curriculum and Experience (PACE) research, the same Standard Assessment Task (SAT) was observed in use in three Year 2 classrooms in different local education authorities (LEAs), providing a case study through which the reliability of the system is assessed. It is suggested that the variations in the circumstances and experience of teachers and children were so marked that the system is seriously flawed. The SAT discussed, Science 1 (Sinking and Floating), was dropped from the 1992 programmes after severe criticism: the article questions whether this was the right response and discusses some of the wider issues raised.

Comment. This paper is directed at educational policy-makers and gives evidence which challenges judgements concerning classroom assessment. It is concerned to improve assessment practice. As such it is educational research.

> **Teaching the Holocaust: the relevance of children's perceptions of Jewish culture and identity** Short G (1994) *British Educational Research Journal* 20(4) 393-405
>
> The Holocaust is now part of the history curriculum for all 11-14-year olds in maintained schools in England and Wales. In this paper it is argued that for the Holocaust to be taught effectively, teachers will need to have some idea of how children within this age group perceive Jewish culture and identity. The empirical core of the paper attempts to go some way towards meeting this need. Seventy-two children aged between 12 and 14 were interviewed in order to explore their knowledge of Judaism, the nature of any misconceptions between Judaism and Christianity and their awareness of anti-Semitism. The paper concludes with a discussion of the policy implications of the findings.

Comment. This paper addresses issues of relevance to history teachers and may aid them in their pedagogic decisions in their classrooms. It comes within the definition of educational research.

Chapter Three ON THE KINDS OF RESEARCH IN EDUCATIONAL SETTINGS

Teacher perceptions of their needs as mentors in the context of developing school-based initial teacher education. Williams A (1993) *British Educational Research Journal* 19 (4) 407-420.

Responses from teachers to a limited investigation of their perceived training needs as potential mentors are analysed in the context of a model which identifies different approaches to mentoring and different level of operation. The diverse views presented by these teachers have implications for future initial teacher education programmes if students are to continue to have access to a wide range of aspects of support and advice.

Comment. This paper clearly has implications for the decisions of teacher trainers. It is an example of educational research.

Value-added attacks: technical issues in reporting national curriculum assessments. Wiliam D (1992) *British Educational Research Journal* 18 (4) 329-341

In 1987 the British government announced its intention to introduce a national curriculum for all students of compulsory school age, with formal assessment being carried out at the ages of seven, 11, 14 and 16, and reported on a common 10-point scale. The assumptions underlying the 10-point scale are examined, as is the way in which criterion-referencing is embodied in the assessment system. Implications of such a model for reporting the attainment of whole cohorts of students are examined and different ways of operationalising the idea of 'value-added' and their relative fairness are explored. Finally, implications about reporting and publishing aggregated school results are drawn for schools and local education authorities.

Comment. This paper is about educational judgements and sets out to suggest effective ways of reporting on assessment. It is educational research.

Group child interviews as a research tool. Lewis A (1992) *British Educational Research Journal* 18 (4) 413-421

Group interviews have several advantages over individual interviews. In particular they help to reveal consensus views, may generate richer responses by allowing participants to challenge one another's views, may be used to verify research ideas or data gained through other methods and may enhance the reliability of children's responses. There are, however, difficulties in carrying out group interviews and they require skilful and sensitive guidance by the interviewer. There have been few reports of their use with primary-aged children but the work reported here suggests that they are a viable and useful technique with that age group.

Comment. This is a methodological paper, discussing a particular approach to data collection. It may influence the decisions of educational researchers in investigating some educational action. As such I suggest it is a paper in the field of educational research, although it could also be claimed by social psychologists.

> **Underachievement: a case of conceptual confusion.** Plewis I (1991) *British Educational Research Journal* 17 (4) 377-385
>
> Although the word underachievement is frequently encountered in educational writing, it is not a well-defined concept. This paper presents alternative operationalisations of underachievement, one based on a discrepancy between attainment and IQ and generally used by psychologists, the other based on relative position and used more by sociologists. Particular attention is paid to technical aspects of the psychologists' definition, and it is shown that an apparently straightforward approach based on a regression model has many drawbacks. The paper ends by suggesting that educational researchers consider dropping underachievement from their vocabulary.

This paper has a philosophical approach which focuses on educational judgements about the value of a particular concept. It is clearly a piece of educational research as defined above.

3. A DEFINITION OF SOCIOLOGICAL RESEARCH IN EDUCATION

Having staked out the ground for educational research, where does this leave the sociologists working in an educational setting? Their concerns are to construct new theoretical understandings, or to develop or to challenge existing ones, in relation to the expectations and existing theories of sociological knowledge. They are trying to make descriptions, analyses, interpretations and explanations in accord with the canons of their discipline. Those who call themselves 'educational sociologists' have chosen to work in an educational setting in order to achieve these ends, but if their work is effective it will rank with other sociological research conducted in other social settings. Thus a suitable definition for this kind of research is this:

> **Sociological research in education aims critically to inform understandings of social phenomena in educational settings.**

Some examples follow.

> **Teachers' careers and comprehensive school closure: policy and professionalism in practice.** Riseborough G F (1994) *British Educational Research Journal* 20(1), 85-104
>
> This paper presents tape-recorded material obtained from ethnographic interviews conducted with two secondary school teachers in an urban working-class school. It illustrates how their careers were made and unmade during a particular historical moment, exploring the experience of the closure of a comprehensive school in the context of falling rolls and monetarist state policy. The collapse of their

(and others') vertical, horizontal and moral careers is presented. The teachers' crises of motivation are outlined, together with the practical accomplishment of transfer to other schools within the authority. In conclusion, the social class position of these teachers is explored - whether their experience pushed them ideologically and culturally closer to their students and the working-class and away from the New Right state and its policy.

Comment. This paper is concerned with social phenomena - with careers, institutional closure, crises of motivation, social class and the New Right. It provides insights which could be linked with studies of these phenomena conducted in other settings, for example factories, regiments or football clubs, to create or comment on macro theories. On the other hand it gives little guidance to inform the practical decisions of anyone engaged in closing a school. It would evoke the sympathy of an administrator, but not offer much help. This is not a negative criticism, but a statement of the intent of the author. It is sociological research in education, not educational research.

What happens when a school subject undergoes a sudden change of status? Paechter C (1993) *Curriculum Studies* 1(3), 349-363

This paper reports some of the findings of the first year of a study of the development of the design and technology curriculum in England and Wales. The establishment of a new, high status, practical subject area offers a unique opportunity to study curriculum history as it happens. Furthermore, as the new subject is being taught by teachers from previously gendered areas, the relationship between gender, power and subject status is particularly illuminated in this context. The paper considers what has happened to the subject area as a result of its elevation to extended core status in the English and Welsh National Curriculum, in terms of both subject and teacher status. A particular focus is the increased academic nature and masculinisation of the subject as a result of its increased status. It is argued that the interaction of gender with power and status is an important but largely ignored aspect of curriculum history.

Comment. Again this paper is concerned with social phenomena: with gender, power and status. It is about a curriculum issue in schools, but is not aimed directly to influence the judgements and decisions of other curriculum planners. Its prime claim to knowledge is in its contribution to understanding across all aspects of society, of gender in relation to power and status. As such, in my view, it is sociological research in education although clearly a claim could be made by historians that it contributes to understanding of educational history because of its focus on a particular curriculum.

Governors, Schools and the Miasma of the Market Deem R, Brehony K, and Heath S (1994) *British Educational Research Journal* 20(5) 535-549

The paper examines some of the effects of exposing state schools to the strictures of the market on three governing bodies of secondary schools in two local education authorities. Using illustrative data drawn from an intensive 4 year study, the authors argue that the imposition of the market on schools can exacerbate value divisions between governors in the same school. Also the concern to improve the image and marketability of a school can result in attention being focused on the needs of future rather than existing pupils. Competition between schools may thus result not in higher quality education or diversity of provision but rather produce a search for uniformity in the shape of the desirable middle-class parent and child. The notion of schools serving a local community may thus be disrupted and choice for working-class and ethnic minority parents and pupils reduced rather than increased.

Comment. A challenging study of the consequences of the political ideology that market forces lead to improvement in schools must surely be sociological research since the prime focus is the social phenomena discovered when this ideology is explored in three schools. Alternatively it could be argued that studies like this could have an effect on the judgements of national policy makers and result in the market forces ideology being abandoned! In this event it would be policy-oriented educational research. Perhaps this example shows that my attempt to distinguish between different kinds of research in educational settings can be problematic.

4. A DEFINITION OF PSYCHOLOGICAL RESEARCH IN EDUCATION

Sociologists are not the only academics working in educational settings who are not engaging in the decisions-and-judgements-to-improve-educational-action type of research which I have defined as educational research. Some psychologists are also working in educational settings and striving to construct new, and challenge existing, theoretical understandings in relation to psychological knowledge. They are working in accord with the canons of their discipline. Those who see themselves as 'educational-psychological researchers' have chosen to work in an educational setting in order to achieve these ends. Thus a suitable definition for this kind of research is this:

Psychological research in education aims critically to inform understandings of psychological phenomena in educational settings.

Again some examples may help to illustrate the argument.

Arguing for yourself: identity as an organising principle in teachers' jobs and lives. Maclure M (1993) *British Educational Research Journal* 19 (4) 311-322

> Biography and life history are currently enjoying a revival in educational research and development. This article considers the implications of adopting a 'biographical attitude' to research and policy issues, and explores the notion of identity as an organising principle in teachers' jobs and lives. Identity, it is suggested, can be seen as a kind of argument - a resource that people use to explain, justify and make sense of themselves in relation to others, and to the world at large. While identity is a site of permanent struggle for everyone, teachers may be undergoing a particularly acute crisis of identity, as the old models and exemplars of teacherhood disintegrate under contemporary social and economic pressures. The article is based upon an empirical study of 69 primary and secondary teachers.

Comment. This is about the psychological concept of 'identity' and is an account of crisis phenomena which it is argued is currently experienced by numbers of teachers. It does not aim to offer insights into educational decisions or judgements which could improve educational action. As such it seems to come within the definition of psychological research in education.

> **Computer anxiety in primary schoolchildren and university students** Todman J and Lawrenson H (1992) *British Educational Research Journal* 18(1) 63-72
> A group of 20 first-year psychology students and a group of 29 nine-year-old children of comparable intelligence completed self-report inventories measuring computer anxiety (CA), mathematics anxiety (MA), trait anxiety (TA) and computer experience (CE). The contributions of age, sex, TA and CE to scores on CA and MA were investigated in multivariate and univariate analyses of covariance. The children were less anxious about computers than the students. The children had higher CE scores than the students, but this difference did not account for the students' higher levels of CA. MA was related to TA and, for students only, MA was higher for females. The results were interpreted as encouraging indications of the absence of a strong link between CA and MA, with the former showing signs of reduction as early experience with computers becomes the norm.

Comment. This is about psychological concepts of 'anxiety'. It does not seem to offer insights into educational decisions or judgements which could improve educational action, but examines relationships between different kinds of anxiety and experience. As such it comes within the definition of psychological research in education rather than of educational research.

5. OTHER DISCIPLINARY RESEARCHES IN EDUCATION

In addition to sociological and psychological enquiries in educational settings there are other disciplinary forms of enquiry, for example historical, philosophical and economic. In my view the following paper is an example of historical research in education.

The curriculum for English 15-year-old pupils in 1984. Was there a common core of subjects? Bell J F (1990) *British Educational Research Journal* 16 (1) 41-52

In this paper, the subject uptake of the pupils who took part in the 1984 Assessment of Performance Unit (APU) Age 15 Science Survey is described. More than 200 different subject names were listed by the pupils, but more than half were studied by just a handful of pupils. The most common subjects, in descending order of frequency, were English, mathematics, geography, history, art, French, physics, biology and chemistry. The sex-related and ability-related differences in uptake are described for the more common subjects and for some of the commonest combinations of subjects. Detailed accounts of the uptakes of science subjects and modern foreign languages are also given.

As a final example I suggest that the following paper is essentially philosophical enquiry because it is concerned with fallibilist and absolutist epistemologies in mathematical education. Its claim to knowledge is that it opens up a new field of enquiry rather than aim to influence the judgements of teachers of mathematics.

Alternative perspectives of the nature of mathematics and their influence on the teaching of mathematics. Lerman S (1990) *British Educational Research Journal* 16 (1) 53-61

This article reports on a doctoral dissertation that examined the current state in the philosophy of mathematics, with a view to identifying possible connections with, and influences upon, mathematics education. Recent work in the sociology of knowledge, proposing a strong case for fallibilist epistemology, can be seen as one perspective, counterposed against absolutist epistemologies. It is proposed that these two views are reflected in the practice of mathematics education, in teaching, research and attitudes to current issues. A field study was carried out, not to provide empirical support but to examine some of the consequences of the theoretical framework proposed, and part of this is described. Finally, some implications of the research are discussed.

6. EDUCATIONAL ACTION RESEARCH

Educational action research is a subset of educational research as defined above. Certainly it 'aims critically to inform educational judgements and decisions in order to improve educational action', but it differs from other kinds of educational research in that it is research carried out by the actors themselves. It is what John Elliott has called 'insider' research. It is research carried out by practitioners to improve their own practice. Personal theory is created not as an end in itself, but in order to advance practice. The topics of enquiry, methods of data collection, analytical techniques, and styles of presenting findings (if communicated at all) reflect the pragmatic needs of teachers and educational managers. The intended audience may be no one other than the researcher, but may also be fellow teachers engaged in similar

Chapter Three ON THE KINDS OF RESEARCH IN EDUCATIONAL SETTINGS

teaching, or fellow managers engaged in similar practice. The researcher in this kind of enquiry may find little in the education literature to guide the enquiries and may need to invent procedures grounded in practice in order to pursue the research.

Action research is often cyclical, because striving for improvement is seen by many practitioners (teachers, teacher-managers, administrators etc) as an ongoing professional commitment.

Because action research entails an intention to change action involving people who are well known to the researcher, it is seen to demand not only a strong ethic of respect for persons, but also democratic involvement of those on whom it impinges. Thus openness, participation of others, and negotiation about the ownership of data and about the uses that the researcher may put it to, are deemed important.

Because they are 'insiders', action researchers are involved emotively as well as cognitively in their enquiries and so it is important to them that their research judgements and decisions are open to challenge. Thus criticism is important, for example as a means of testing whether findings represent what they purport to represent. To this end the action researchers have embraced the concept of the 'critical friend', meaning someone who responds to the invitation to invest some time and effort into critically examining a colleague's action research procedures and findings, and who agrees to work within the ethical framework of the enquiry - which defines matters such as the ownership of data.

Action research is a strategy for inducing change and the following three examples illustrate this.

(a) **The management of children in the dining room at lunch-time.** Busby S (1991) (In Lomax, P (ed) *Managing better schools and colleges: an action research way*, BERA Dialogues, Multilingual Matters, Clevedon, England)

Busby carried out action research in the school year of 1989-90 on the management of children in the dining room at lunch-time in a large multi-ethnic primary school in London where he was a teacher.

The situation that he identified was this:
> The dinner staff were experiencing a great deal of abuse when lining up children on the downstairs corridor. Fights, swearing, kicking, pushing and anti-social behaviour were apparent both in and outside the dining hall. My daily observations showed that the general noise level was high and the ethos of the hall negative, aggressive and unruly and not conducive to good relations, respect or good lunch habits. ... It was apparent to me that the

whole business of lunch-hour supervision needed attention as it was clearly on a knife-edge daily and could easily swing completely out of control for the dinner staff.

This was in conflict with his own beliefs and those of his colleagues about the potential value of school meal time, as expressed in these words:

> My own belief is that the lunch break is a special communal and sharing time of the day. At such times table manners, conversation, togetherness and community are all of great importance and are part of the personal and social education programme of the school.

His research questions were:

(i)   how can the management of the children in the dining room be improved;
(ii) how can the morale of the dinner ladies be raised and they be trained in child management; and
(iii) how can the teachers help change the ethos of the hall at lunch-time?

Through a cyclical, systematic and critical process of observation, conversation, questionnaire, meetings, innovation, and evaluation, which involved all of the participants - children, dinner ladies, headteacher, other teachers and himself - the situation improved. Also the 'ownership' of the project changed, as he describes in these words:

> The project, which in many ways had started off as an initiative from me, became adopted by others and left my hands to be steered and re-planned by the dinner ladies themselves for they had been awakened to fresh needs. They wanted to carry on themselves as they had found they could succeed in their own right. I take this to show that the ownership of the project was passed to others who enthusiastically wanted to carry on themselves shaping it in the ways they felt best.

Comment. The obvious value of this research was to the school in reducing the severity of a problem. The publication of the report however serves several other ends, for example: (1) at a practical level, showing to other schools that it is possible for school dinner-time problems to be reduced in severity; and (2) at a theoretical level, adding to the evidence of the power of innovations which are owned by those who introduce them.

(b)   **The implementation and evaluation of a drama course for all secondary pupils in a comprehensive school** Rushworth L (1993) in Turner, D (ed) *Research in action*, Pavic Publications, Sheffield, England

Chapter Three ON THE KINDS OF RESEARCH IN EDUCATIONAL SETTINGS

Rushworth conducted an enquiry into the teaching of drama in a secondary school where she was a member of the English department. The boundary around this study of a singularity was all 2nd and 3rd year pupils in the school and the three English teachers who were responsible for teaching them drama, in the school year 1988/9. The research question was the issue of whether replacing one of five English lessons per week by a drama lesson was educationally justifiable. Data was collected by questionnaire for pupils and interview with staff. The findings show that 57 of the 88 pupils 'felt that they had definitely benefited from taking drama since it had developed their communicative and social skills' (p63) and all three members of staff considered the innovation worthwhile. Various problems were identified, for example, 21 pupils did not believe GCSE Drama was a worthwhile qualification and 24 indicated that they did not feel they were any good at drama.

Comment. The most obvious value of this research was within the school, in seeking justification for an innovation and in identifying aspects which needed attention. The merit of publishing the report is (1) that by example it may encourage other schools to experiment with drama for all and to conduct research on its value and problems, and (2) when someone, somewhere, writes a review of drama teaching in schools, this isolated instance may be combined with others to help formulate an overview of the teaching of drama which may, perhaps, influence future policy.

(c)   **Language counts in the teaching of mathematics** Wright, S (1990) in Webb, R (ed) *Practitioner research in the primary school,* Falmer Press, Basingstoke, England

Wright was teaching part-time in a five-class primary school where, among other duties, she taught mathematics to twelve middle infants for five sessions a week. Six of these provide the focus of the research. She made a study of their language, her language and the language of the Nuffield Infant Maths Scheme, because of 'a growing awareness of some children's difficulties in coping with the language of maths lessons' (p127). She identified 14 research questions, grouped as follows:

Questioning

What kind of questions do I ask? What kind of questions do the children ask me? What kind of questions do the children ask each other? What kind of questions are asked on the worksheets? What kind of response do the various questions elicit?

Word usage

Which words do the children actually use? How does this compare with the words in the Nuffield lists? Are there any mathematical words which cause particular difficulty? Which words do the children use wrongly? Does my language have any bearing on this?

Shared meanings and misunderstandings

Is there any discernible pattern in the areas of misunderstanding? In which areas is there little or no confusion shown by any of the six children? Can I as a teacher learn anything from this?

Non-linguistic evidence of understanding

What factors other than language indicate comprehension? (pp127-128)

Over a six-month period she taped and transcribed interactions between herself and the six children and between the children on their own on the maths topics of time, length and weight. She also made field notes. The analysis of the transcripts is presented in the research report under these headings: my questions; the children's questions; vocabulary and word usage; confusions and misunderstandings; understanding and share meanings. This analysis raises a large number of issues, many of which are related to the existing literature, as the following two extracts from the report show.

> Even though 'it is a normal feature of classroom discourse that teachers ask a great many questions, and consequently that pupils do a great deal of answering' (Atkinson, 1981, p109) nonetheless, the most striking thing on analysing the transcripts was the comparative infrequency of the children's questions. The topics of time and length contained only 34 children's questions, as opposed to about 500 of mine. However the weighing topic [where the children were on their own part of the time] produced 85 children's questions, 43 of which were addressed to me and 42 to the other children. The fact that variation in data-collection techniques can influence results so dramatically makes one hesitant to draw any firm conclusions from the number of questions asked. (p133)

> Although Simon often rushed through his work making careless mistakes, he did have a good basic understanding and occasional flashes of real insight. When we were looking at the sand timers, before I had started to talk about them at all, he looked at the ten minute one and said:
>
> *Simon:* That goes slow 'cos it's got a little hole.
>
> His lack of facility with words, but his clear comprehension, is shown again in the following extract. We had measured a paintbrush with cubes and then with dominoes:
>
> *Simon:* I know why there's - er - less than the bigger because they're bigger than the them.
>
> (I have double-checked the transcript with the tape: those were his exact words).
>
> *SW:* ... Tell me what you just said, Simon.
> *Simon:* Well, er. I know why that's less than them - because - er - they're bigger.
> *SW:* The dominoes are bigger, so it doesn't take as many.
> *Simon:* Yes.

Kerslake (1982, p79) suggests that:
> Teachers need to adjust to the natural language of the children in the classroom as well as expecting the children to adjust to the more formal language of mathematics.

Children like Simon need a lot of help and encouragement to express their understanding of concepts in a comprehensible way and to move towards 'the more formal language of mathematics'. (pp150-151)

What was the outcome of this research? Wright summarises her main findings in these words:

The findings of the research had implications for improvements in both practice and materials. There should be greater use of reasoning questions by the teacher and more opportunity for children to hypothesise about their work; children's active use of mathematical vocabulary should be encouraged together with an awareness of the need to extend the personal vocabulary of some children; some of the worksheets which caused confusion by their format rather than their conceptual content should be redesigned. (p152)

Comment. The style of the conclusion implies that the audience is no more than Wright herself and a few colleagues, for she says:
> We have been consciously working towards implementing the recommendations we have made, both in our own practice and in disseminating the results of our work among other infant staff. (p152)

By publishing the report however, she potentially achieves much more. (1) Many primary school teachers could be stimulated to reflect on their own practice by reading this report and might, for example, be encouraged to focus their statutory appraisal on the ways in which, in conversations with children, they try to bridge the gap between the natural language of the children and the formal language of say mathematics: a consequence might be the enhancement of the quality of this activity. (2) Theorists might find challenge or support for their ideas from the detailed descriptions she gives of her interaction with children and, combining these with data from other studies, for example extend the contention of Kerslake to which she refers.

7. DISCUSSION

It is not always clear-cut as to which kind of research in education a particular study belongs, and no doubt some of my judgements made above may be challenged by others. Many research papers can be fitted into this typology, as I have tried to show, but there are likely to be problems arising from papers that 'don't fit', perhaps because they embrace more than one kind of research in education.

But I claim that the recognition of these different kinds of research in education effectively counters the criticism that Lord Skidelsky, at the beginning of this chapter, made when he said that 'education is an immature discipline' and 'there is no theoretically based good practice which defines professional teaching.'

Within the arena that I am describing as educational research, the concept of 'theory' is quite different from that of sociologists, psychologists, philosophers, historians, or economists. There are few general theories. Instead there are personal theories of practitioners and of policy-makers. Piaget, for example, is no longer significant. Gone are the days when the 'gurus' were Froebel, or Montessori, or Arnold, or Newman. Yet some of their ideas, merged with aspects of constructivist learning theory and theories of motivation and social dynamics, will be found in the personal theories of individuals. The competent teacher of today has a complex pattern of understandings that come partly from training and from reading, but largely from experience and from professional discourse with colleagues. Some are taking their understanding forward through personal action research, the development of which is probably the greatest achievement of all time of educational research. Educational research, seen as informing educational judgements and decisions in order to improve educational action, serves practitioners and policy-makers by contributing to the development of their personal theories, and in the process may serve other researchers by building frameworks for them to extend further.

I would add one further thought. I suspect that research into education is similar to research into management, health care, social work, criminology, and prison studies, in its paucity of general theory, but focus on personal theory that underpins practice and policy. I guess that, for example, there is a whole arena of management research which aims critically to inform management judgements and decisions in order to improve management action. And likewise there will be sociological research in management and psychological research in management which aim critically to inform understandings of social and psychological phenomena in management settings. Teasing these out for each of the professional studies listed above would help to clarify, across the social sciences, the legitimate roles of different kinds of researchers and, hopefully, clear the way for the development of parity of esteem between them.

Chapter Four

ON THE PROCESS OF RESEARCH IN EDUCATION

Sections

1.	ASKING RESEARCH QUESTIONS	54
2.	THE PROCESS OF EMPIRICAL ENQUIRY	57

When the Festival of Britain of 1951 in London on the South Bank of the Thames closed, there was concern about pilfering and extra police were drafted in to supervise the exits from the site. The story is told of one London bobby who became suspicious about a particular individual who kept leaving the site with a wheelbarrow piled high with straw. Time after time he searched the straw to see if anything was hidden in it but never found anything. Years later, after he had retired from the force, he happened to meet the same man in a pub and, after several drinks, asked him what it was that he had been taking. 'Well,' said the man, 'you were asking the wrong question - you were searching the straw. It was wheelbarrows that I was nicking!'

In carrying out any search for truth, it is necessary to ask the right questions. In my experience too many researchers have a tendency to plunge into data collection before they have clarified what research questions they are asking. In this chapter I first set out some of the ideas which I have formulated on the asking of research questions and then describe an idealised research process for empirical enquiry which I have used over a number of years with master's students engaging in research.

1. ASKING RESEARCH QUESTIONS

In carrying out research the purpose is to try to make some claim to knowledge; to try to show something that was not known before. Thus the starting point of research is asking the question 'What claim to knowledge am I trying to make?' Appropriately framed, this becomes the *research question*. Some writers on research insist that the starting point must be a hypothesis, but I find this too limiting. I believe there are three major forms of expressing an enquiry, each of which leads to research questions. The three are: the research hypothesis, the research problem, and the research issue.

Some research starts straightaway with a sharp focus expressed in a clearly expressed *hypothesis*. The next step is to devise the research questions which will enable it to be tested. Other research has a more blurred focus, such as a *problem* to be tackled, or an *issue* to be explored, where some simple research questions may need to be asked before more pertinent ones can be formulated.

This categorisation deserves elaboration. It is not a rigid, three-fold classification of mutually exclusive possibilities, but a set of categories which can help define the immediate purpose of a research enquiry. Often a research intention can be expressed under more than one of these headings by juggling the words describing it, but nevertheless one of the three may be judged to be the most suitable way of describing the research at a particular stage of enquiry.

A *research hypothesis* is a tentative statement or conjecture that is in a form which can be tested. It enables clear research questions to be asked which should provide evidence which either supports the hypothesis or refutes it. The research purpose is to test the hypothesis. Karl Popper taught that it is more valuable to seek evidence which may challenge an hypothesis than may support it, because an unsuccessful challenge increases confidence in the validity of the hypothesis.

A *research problem* identifies a difficulty which often can be expressed as a contradiction between what is happening and what someone would like to happen. The simple idea that where there is a problem the job of the researcher is to find a solution, is usually unrealistic. The research purpose is more likely to be to formulate and try out ways in which the problem may be better understood and so be alleviated or the difficulty reduced, and to this end appropriate research questions need to be asked. Sometimes a research problem in educational research may be best addressed by a two-stage format of research questions of this kind:

> *What is happening in this educational process now?*
> *How can we try to improve it?*

This is a format particularly useful for teachers and other practitioners who engage in action research.

A *research issue* is the least defined category of research. It describes an area for enquiry, where no problems or hypotheses have yet been clearly expressed that will direct the enquiry. The research purpose here is to strive to focus the issue through asking pertinent research questions.

These three categories of research are illustrated in figure [1].

In each case *research questions* define specific data to be obtained. A research question clearly sets the agenda for research and enables data to be collected and analysis started. In defining the research question it is important to establish the boundaries in space and time of the enquiry. For example: which learners, or teachers, or institutions, are the focus of the enquiry and at what time? If a claim to knowledge is subsequently made, it refers, of course, to the space and time within this boundary.

Figure [1]   **Examples of a research issue, a research problem and a research hypothesis - each leading to research questions**

Research issue: An enquiry into reading in this school.

This is as yet a broad field of enquiry. It could lead to **research questions** like 'how do our children's reading standards compare with other schools now' and 'what processes of learning to read are used by our children in and out of school at present?' This might lead to the identification of some problems which could be the subject of further research.

Research problem: The children in this school are not learning to read as effectively as the teachers would wish. Could their parents assist in the process?

This enquiry as yet has only a blurred focus, i.e. that there is a gap between pupil performance and teacher expectation. A possible way in which this gap might be reduced has been put forward and it is now necessary to pose **research questions** such as 'what could our parents do now to assist' and 'why might this improve our children's reading abilities?' This might entail reading the literature, enquiring about practices in neighbouring schools, and seeking the views of parents. The outcome of these enquiries might be that a read-once-a-day-to-your-child scheme would be tried - and at some stage tested to see how well it works.

Research hypothesis: That the children of classes four and five of this school whose parents participated in the read-once-a-day-to-your-child scheme during last year, will have gained more in reading age over the year than those whose parents have not participated.

This is a more sophisticated research enquiry than the previous one. It can now be re-expressed as three **research questions**: 'to what extent did each of the children of classes four and five of this school participate in the parental read-once-a-day-to-your-child scheme during the past year'; 'what is the gain in reading age of each child in these classes in week six of this term compared to a year ago'; and 'is there a causal relationship between these answers?'

2. THE PROCESS OF EMPIRICAL ENQUIRY

This section describes the typical process of an empirical enquiry, meaning research where conclusions are based predominantly on data collected by the researcher(s) by asking questions of people, and observing events, etc. This process is described here in terms of six stages. Although set out in sequence, it is not always the case that one follows the previous one exactly - sometimes these develop in parallel and sometimes they are repeated in a cyclical process. Many researchers find it helpful to prepare an action plan for such a research enquiry, indicating roughly how long will be spent on different stages of the study and when they will occur. Experience shows that often data analysis requires more time than data collection, and report writing even longer. Action plans need to be seen as tentative documents which are regularly rewritten.

Formulating the research question

First, having identified a research issue, or problem, or hypothesis, the researcher needs to write down one or more research questions, as described above. As the research develops it is likely that there will be changes in the way the research questions are expressed.

Conceptual background

Secondly is an examination of the conceptual, or theoretical, background to the enquiry. What is the state of existing knowledge? Every piece of research has a theoretical background and it is an important part of the systematic approach for the researcher to articulate this background.

It is useful in educational research to recognise that there are two kinds of theory available in many cases to the researcher: theory-in-the-literature and common-sense theory of practitioners.

Theory-in-the-literature is the knowledge which has been published in the literature and which is thus available for researchers to read and base their expectations on. Studying this enables the research to be located in the context of other studies and is likely to influence the design of the enquiry.

Common-sense theory is the hitherto unrecorded knowledge of practitioners (for example, teachers), which may well include the researcher. It may be thought of as knowledge-in-action, because it is the kind of knowledge which underpins much of the action of practitioners, but which has not been effectively expressed in writing. Until recently few academics were prepared to recognise the existence of common-sense theory as a possible starting point for research. Of course, once it has been written down and published in a research paper it moves into the realm of theory-in-the-literature and its credibility will depend upon the evidence assembled to support it.

Let me give an illustration of common-sense theory. A student working with me had chosen to study, as an issue, the educational benefits of infants making collages. She could find no research papers on this topic and the school art books which dealt with collage gave no more than practical hints on what kind of things children might do. Failing to find any theory-in-the-literature this student put together a common-sense theory, from her own experience and from that of several teachers with whom she talked. She expressed this in terms of manipulative experiences (with scissors), mathematics (in terms of shapes), language (in terms of oral expressions), social experience (in terms of sharing the materials) and aesthetic experience (in terms of the process of making something satisfying). This common-sense theory was then tested out in a classroom, to see the extent to which children with whom she was working actually gained some of these benefits.

Method

Thirdly comes a consideration of the method of the enquiry. What methods of data collection are being chosen and why these and not others? What are the advantages and what are the limitations? Are they well-tried methods, with a theory of their own, or are they home-spun methods devised by the researcher in terms of common-sense theory of enquiry? This is part of the self-critical aspect of research, where the researcher needs to examine carefully his/her decisions about how the enquiry is conducted. It is usual in a pedagogic study (meaning a student's assignment, special study or dissertation - see the discussion in the next chapter) for the researcher not only to give an account of why a particular method was chosen, but, after the data has been collected and analysed, to give a detailed criticism of the method in the light of having used it. In an academic study (meaning one by an experienced researcher) this is in the mind, but not articulated in print.

Data collection

Fourthly is the process of data collection, of using the chosen methods of enquiry to amass relevant facts, of collecting them systematically and storing them carefully, of looking at each piece of data critically and asking of it, is this what it purports to be? Questions to ask here are: is the data appropriate for its intended purpose; is sufficient data being collected (but not too much - William of Occam in the 14th century said: 'it is vain to do with more what can be done with less'); is the process of collecting the data ethical in terms of respect for persons and of respect for truth?

Data analysing and interpreting

The fifth stage is the analysis of the data, of sifting it to find patterns, of trying to condense it into manageable proportions, of trying to interpret it, and of reflecting on its meanings. As described below, at this stage it may be appropriate to refocus the enquiry, rewrite the research question, and start the research process again.

Making a claim to knowledge

The final stage is to express lucidly and cogently, and with an audience in mind, what it is that has been found out and why it is believed to be the case.

Linear research and cyclical research

Linear research is a term which I use to describe the process of having one stab at a hypothesis, problem or issue. The investigation is planned; it is implemented and data collected; the data is analysed, interpreted, and conclusions drawn; the whole process is then critically reflected on; and finally, a report prepared.

By contrast, cyclical research involves a continuing process in which designing an investigation, carrying it out, analysing the results, and reflecting on it is but the first cycle, providing an interim report. On the basis of this first report the focus may be redefined and a new round of investigations carried out in an attempt to get closer to whatever truth is being sought. In this cyclical process the direction of the research may change quite radically when a set of findings causes a rethink. This is illustrated in figure [2].

Carrying out a pilot study in order to try out research methods prior to conducting a larger scale study is an example of two-stage cyclical research. Classroom action research usually uses a cyclical approach.

Intervention and non-intervention studies

Intervention research is where some change is introduced into the existing situation and the consequences are studied. For example a new teaching procedure may be tried out with a class, or a novel management procedure in a school, and the changed situation is monitored and the outcomes evaluated.

Non-intervention research is where no change is made but where the existing situation is studied. For example a well established teaching procedure may be monitored and analysed.

An experiment is obviously an intervention because it entails something novel, whereas a survey is likely to be concerned with an existing situation and is thus a non-intervention form of research.

It can be argued, of course, that the very act of studying an existing situation is an intervention, because something different from normal is happening. If obtrusive observers or domineering video cameras are in use, or if such thought-provoking questions are being asked that participants change their work patterns, then there is substance to this argument. However when researchers collect data discretely, and maintain a low profile in relation to the ongoing action, I take the view that the designation 'non-intervention' research is appropriate.

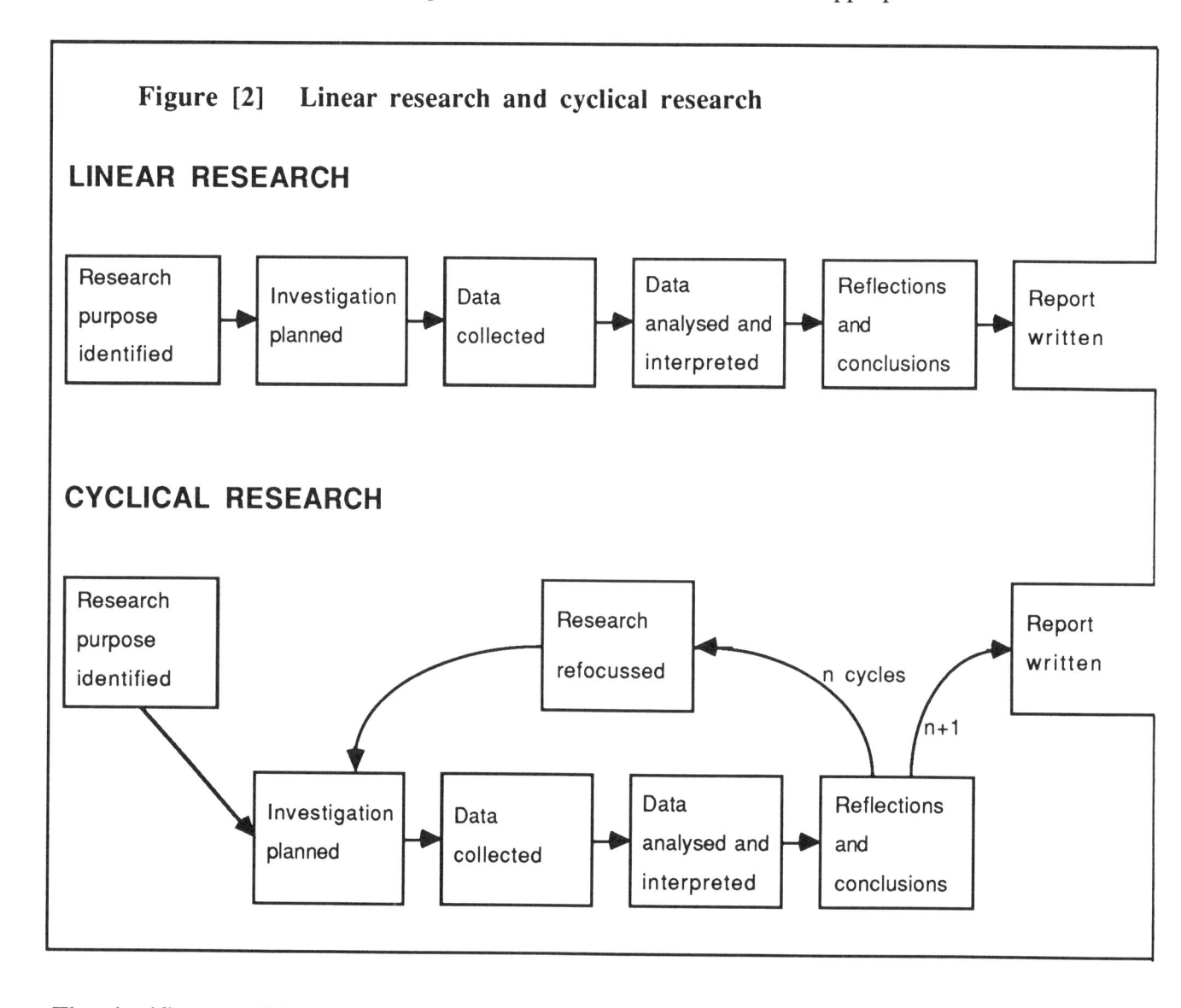

Figure [2] Linear research and cyclical research

LINEAR RESEARCH

Research purpose identified → Investigation planned → Data collected → Data analysed and interpreted → Reflections and conclusions → Report written

CYCLICAL RESEARCH

Research purpose identified → Investigation planned → Data collected → Data analysed and interpreted → Reflections and conclusions; from Reflections and conclusions, n cycles back to Research refocussed → Investigation planned; after n+1, Report written.

The significance of these terms arises in terms of the ethics of the enquiry. Both kinds of enquiry entail negotiation with those who provide data about its ownership, but in addition an intervention enquiry requires negotiation to ensure that the intervention is acceptable in terms of those who will be involved.

Planning research

The ideas expressed above lead to twelve questions about the planning of a research enquiry, as set out in Figure [3]. Some of these are difficult questions to answer. Often it is not easy to see the paradigm which is influencing one's work, but the exercise of trying to decide may reveal factors which have hitherto been latent. Trying to answer question (4) by identifying the claim to educational knowledge which it is hoped will arise from the research, is rejected by some people on the grounds that 'on a voyage of discovery how can I know where I'm going until I arrive there', to which a suitable answer is 'Colombus was seeking a new route to India when he discovered America.' The mistake is not in being expected to have an aim, but in being inflexible in redefining that aim when the data so requires. Likewise those who reject question (4) because 'preconceived ideas will cloud my judgement' need to recognise that the systematic, critical and self-critical nature of research is fundamental to the dispersal of clouds of unwisdom.

Figure [3]   A questionary for planning empirical research

(1)   What is the research question at this stage? Is the starting point a research hypothesis, a research problem, or a research issue? Is the enquiry envisaged as a linear study or a cyclical study?

(2)   Is this a search to understand; or to understand and evaluate; or to understand, evaluate and try to change? Are you working as an 'insider' or an 'outsider'?

(3)   Is it a study of a singularity or a search for a generalisation? Is the enquiry located in the positivist paradigm or the interpretive paradigm? Are the implications of the answers to these clear?

(4)   What kind of claim to educational knowledge is it hoped will arise from the research?

(5)   Has an action plan been prepared showing when and where stages of the research, such as data collection, data analysis, and report writing, will occur? Has sufficient time been allocated?

Figure [3] (continued)

(6) Has an ethical statement been prepared?

(7) What conceptual background is the starting point of this research? Is it theory-in-the-literature, or common-sense theory, or both?

(8) What methods of data collection and data analysis will be used? Are they taken, or adapted from, the literature, or based on common-sense theory?

(9) Will the collection of data, as planned, be likely to be appropriate, sufficient, and ethical? Are there adequate resources and sufficient time for data collection? Is access to data assured? How will it be stored? Will a critical friend be involved?

(10) Will the analysis of data, as planned, be likely to be appropriate, sufficient, and ethical? Does the planning give sufficient time for data analysis, data interpretation and for reflection? Will a critical friend be involved?

(11) Is the research to be reported in the academic mode, the professional mode or the pedagogic mode? Will the report be in the structured style or the narrative style? [These terms are discussed in the next chapter] Has sufficient time for writing been allowed? Will a critical friend be involved? Who will be the audience?

(12) Is the overall design of the research, as set out in answers to these questions, likely to succeed in making the hoped for claim to educational knowledge?

A device which I have sometimes found helpful in trying to answer question four, is to write a 'potential abstract'. This is a piece of fictional writing which represents what I envisage being able to write when the data has been collected and analysed. It means that the boundaries surrounding the hoped for claim to knowledge have to be delineated, and sometimes this helps to show whether too much, or too little, data is being planned for. Of course, the research may take a different course to that planned and the actual abstract may be very different from its progenitor. The next chapter contains a discussion of what may constitute an abstract and may be of help in preparing a 'potential abstract'.

Chapter Five

ON THE WRITING OF RESEARCH IN EDUCATION

Sections

1.	MODES OF REPORTING RESEARCH	64
2.	STRUCTURED REPORTING AND NARRATIVE REPORTING	66
3.	PERSONAL AND IMPERSONAL STYLES OF WRITING	67
4.	FRAMEWORK FOR MAKING A CRITIQUE OF A RESEARCH PAPER	68
5.	ON WRITING EMPIRICAL RESEARCH REPORTS IN EDUCATION	69
6.	SOME FLAWS AND FRIPPERIES IN RESEARCH PAPERS	76
7.	REFERENCING SYSTEMATICALLY	79
8.	ON WRITING REFLECTIVE RESEARCH PAPERS IN EDUCATION	82
9.	WRITING FOR THE READER LUCIDLY AND COGENTLY	84

The poet, writing to a friend, ended the letter saying 'I apologise for writing at such length; I didn't have time to write more briefly'. I suspect that something similar is true of much research writing: that researchers give too little time to the arduous business of writing. Criticising others while struggling myself to write lucidly, I can hear the cynics saying 'Physician first heal thyself'. Nevertheless I will register my complaint. In my view, the standard of much research writing in education is poor. This arises from my own reading of journal articles and, as a referee, of papers submitted to a number of journals, and is strengthened by discussion with several journal editors who report that referees reject substantial proportions of the papers submitted to them for publication.

This chapter brings together a number of ideas on research writing that I have explored in workshops with researchers in training. Of these the most fundamental, which surely should be the most obvious, is that one is writing for an audience and the needs of that audience require careful consideration if the communication is to be effective.

1. MODES OF REPORTING RESEARCH

The publication of research in education comes in many different forms and I find it to be a helpful construct to refer to three modes called the academic, the professional and the pedagogic modes of reporting research. Each is a way of describing research and presenting its findings, but they have different audiences that make different demands on the writer. Recognition of these differences can be particularly helpful to a student working on an assignment, special study, dissertation, or thesis, in showing why the demands being made on him or her by the tutor are different from the demands made on the tutor in writing a paper for an academic journal, or in writing an article for an educational newspaper.

The academic mode of reporting research

The academic mode is used in academic books, papers written in learned journals, and for papers presented at academic conferences. The purpose is to contribute to educational knowledge from an academic stance, i.e. to add to theory-in-the-literature. The audience is other researchers and in writing the paper the author is expected to display not only the findings of the research, with sufficient description of the method of enquiry so that academic readers can examine critically the basis of the findings, but also to give a carefully documented account of how the claim to knowledge fits in with the relevant existing literature. There are many conventions for academic publication that reflect the systematic expectations of research; in particular, journals tend to have their own 'house styles' in terms of presentation of data and citation of the work of others.

Chapter Five ON THE WRITING OF RESEARCH IN EDUCATION

The professional mode of reporting research

The professional mode is used in articles in magazines or newspapers, oral accounts at a conference, or photocopied papers distributed to a few colleagues. The purpose is to contribute to educational knowledge from a professional stance, ie to add to practical knowledge. The audience is teachers (or others engaged in the educational service) and in preparing the publication the author needs to find effective and brief ways of presenting findings so that they can be understood quickly. The audience is likely to be primarily interested in how the findings can inform their own practice rather than in critically examining the methods used. Sometimes an effective way of presenting research findings is to write one paper for an academic audience and a second paper for a professional audience.

The pedagogic mode of reporting research

The pedagogic mode is used by students writing research assignments, special studies, dissertations and theses. The purpose is to demonstrate to a tutor, and possibly an external examiner, that the student is learning to conduct systematic, critical and self-critical enquiry. Thus, as in the academic mode, the author is expected to display the findings of the research, with sufficient description of the method of enquiry so that academic readers can examine critically the basis of the findings, and to give a carefully documented account of how the claim to knowledge fits in with the relevant existing literature, but also the author is expected to articulate the processes of self-criticism in giving a full account of the chosen methods of

Figure [4]   Three modes of reporting research

MODE	TYPE OF REPORT	LENGTH	AUDIENCE
Academic	paper in a journal	medium	researchers
	book	long	researchers
Professional	article in a magazine	short	teachers
	paper to colleagues	short	teachers
Pedagogic	assignment	short	tutor/examiner
	special study	medium	tutor/examiner
	dissertation/thesis	long	tutor/examiner

enquiry. However, unlike the academic mode, the student is not necessarily expected to make a significant claim to knowledge, except in the case of a PhD thesis and to a lesser extent an MPhil or MEd dissertation.

2. STRUCTURED REPORTING AND NARRATIVE REPORTING

Research reports often read as though the researchers knew from the start exactly what they were setting out to do and moved in a linear direction towards that end. This I call 'structured reporting'. Actually research is rarely like this, but it is a recognised convention that reports may be written in this way. The merit of the approach is that the reader can take a short cut through the meanderings taken by the researchers and get quickly to the essence of the claim to knowledge and learn how it was substantiated.

Structured reporting

Structured reports of educational research in academic journals tend to follow a pattern like this. First there may be an abstract - most journals require this as part of their 'house style'. Second comes an introduction to the paper which probably indicates the claim to knowledge that is being made as an appetiser, and sets out the background to the study. This usually includes an indication of the perceived importance of the enquiry. Third is a review of relevant theoretical knowledge as recorded in the literature or of the previously unarticulated common sense understandings of teachers about the issue under study. This is written as the 'springboard' from which the enquiry stems. Fourth is an account of the method of enquiry - a statement of how the evidence was collected. Fifth is a section usually entitled 'Results' and sixth comes 'Discussion' in which the results are analysed, interpreted and conclusions drawn. The paper ends with a list of references that have been cited. A more detailed description of one way of writing like this is given later in this chapter.

This time-hallowed procedure is not without its snags. For example the style implies that the literature review is completed before the empirical enquiry starts. It is as though all the papers cited had been read and digested before the investigation was planned. In practice this rarely happens. People start a piece of research because it interests them and while conducting the enquiry read the literature. Occasionally researchers put a footnote to the effect that 'after completing this study a significant paper by Brown and Smith came to our attention' but this is unusual.

An important advantage of the style is that it enables the researchers to omit parts of their work that have ended in cul-de-sacs: the bits which proved irrelevant, or didn't work, or couldn't be finished in the time available. It permits researchers to organise the account of the events in such a way as to present to the reader a logical account of what has been discovered. This does not mean, of course, that structured reporting distorts the truth about the claim to knowledge, but simply means that it involves an attempt to communicate clearly the basis of that claim.

Researchers working in the positivist paradigm nearly always write in this style, those working in the interpretative paradigm may work to this style, or to a more narrative style.

Narrative reporting

The narrative style of report writing tells the story of how the research was conducted. It gives the reader more of an idea of the stages through which the research developed and what decisions were made, but, in consequence, has the disadvantage of being long. The narrative needs to be organised into sections in order to help the reader. Each section probably represents a period of time during which a significant stage of the research was conducted. The sections appear in chronological order and so stage-by-stage the report can show how questions were asked and answers sought, and how hypotheses were tested, found wanting, modified, retested, and so on, while issues may be seen to develop and be refocused in the light of interim findings. A narrative account of research contains the same elements listed above under 'structured style', but instead of teasing these out and writing about each separately, in a 'narrative style' they are intermingled. Although this is the easiest style to write, it is a difficult style to write well. Essentially it is about writing true stories and, as with all story writing, the interest of the audience needs to be held: so, as in structured writing, it may be necessary to decide what to leave out of the total chronology of the research.

3. PERSONAL AND IMPERSONAL STYLES OF WRITING

> I asked the child ...
> The researcher asked the child ...
> The child was asked ...
>
> In my view ...
> In the opinion of the present writer ...

The use of the first person in research reports can be a matter of much contention. It needn't be because it should be quite clear when it is necessary, and when it is unnecessary.

When a chemist takes a test-tube and mixes together acid and chalk it is certain that the personality, manner, or clothing of the person doing it will have no bearing on the release of carbon dioxide. But when a social scientist asks a question, his or her personality, manner and clothing may have a considerable bearing on the giving of an answer. A pin striped man, with an officious voice and a stern manner asking a young girl why she has played truant, is himself likely to be a significant variable affecting the answer given, as would be a sweatshirt-and-jeans woman, with a local accent and a friendly smile asking her the same question.

It follows that the justification for using the first person is simple. If you think you are in any way likely to be a variable in the conduct of the research and conceivably could affect the outcome, then write in the first person. Otherwise you are distorting the reader's understanding of the context of the enquiry.

The justification for using the third person passive is that if you are not likely to be a significant variable, then this simplifies the reader's understanding of the context. In other words the reader doesn't have to bother thinking about you. Your personality or status or appearance are irrelevant and so to mention you would be to clutter the account with insignificant data. The exception to this view is when in a narrative account you feel that the addition of a few apparently irrelevant details of human interest aid the telling of the story. Here it is a matter of personal judgement.

However I can see no justification for the style in which the self is referred to in the third person. Phrases such as 'the present researcher' seem simply pretentious. It is an unworthy linguistic device to make the subjective masquerade as objective!

Where a decision is reported in a piece of research, it is usually helpful to the reader to know who took the decision and why. Consider this sentence.

> It was decided to use questionnaires to collect data rather than to conduct interviews.

Did the researcher decide this (for methodological reasons), or the headteacher of the school (for administrative reasons)? We need to know if, for example, we want to repeat the study.

4. FRAMEWORK FOR MAKING A CRITIQUE OF A RESEARCH PAPER

In searching for ways of helping researchers to consider the reader's perspective, I stress that a reader wants to know what claim to knowledge is being made and what grounds there are for such a claim. Sometimes this is not easy to ascertain - and this I use as one indicator of impoverished writing.

The questions set out in figure [5] give a framework for making a detailed critique of a research paper. If figure [3] represents the producer's guidelines, this figure represents the consumer's perspective. I have used this extensively with students and believe it has been helpful to them in their own writing. The cautionary note is that sometimes it has led my students to become very cynical about the educational literature, by giving them a powerful tool to castigate inadequate research papers!

> **Figure [5] Framework for a critique of a research paper**
>
> (1) What *claim to educational knowledge* is claimed? What advance in knowledge is the author claiming to have made?
>
> (2) What *conceptual background* does the author give for this research?
>
> (3) What *method* underpinned the enquiry?
>
> (4) Was the *collection of data,* as reported, appropriate, sufficient, ethical?
>
> (5) Was the *analysis and interpretation of data,* as reported, appropriate, sufficient, ethical?
>
> (6) Does the evidence of the paper, as examined in answer to questions (2) to (5), *substantiate the claim to knowledge* made in answer to (1)?
>
> (7) Is the *presentation* of the paper such as to enable the above questions to be answered?
>
> (8) Was the enquiry *worthwhile?*

5. ON WRITING EMPIRICAL RESEARCH REPORTS IN EDUCATION

There are many ways in which research reports can be written and to some extent the choice of headings depends upon the content. The following ideas are ones that I have found helpful and are linked to the critique system described in the previous section. They assume that the purpose of writing is to make, and substantiate, a claim to knowledge. The most important idea, of course, is that the structure should help convey the contents to the reader lucidly and cogently: writing is for an audience!

My recommended structure for a paper reporting on an empirical enquiry in educational research is given in figure [6]. This is more detailed than the traditional structure of Introduction, Literature review, Method, Results, and Discussion and I hope the rationale for suggesting it becomes clear in the ensuing paragraphs. Obviously, according to circumstances it may be best to change the headings, or the order of the items.

Figure [6]   Structure for an empirical research paper

TITLE

Authors and location

ABSTRACT

INTRODUCTION

CONCEPTUAL BACKGROUND

METHOD OF ENQUIRY

DATA COLLECTION

DATA ANALYSIS AND INTERPRETATION

EMPIRICAL CONCLUSION

REFLECTIONS or DISCUSSION or GENERAL CONCLUSION

References

Address for correspondence

What goes in the ABSTRACT ?

The abstract should convey to the reader concisely and accurately within the space of a few sentences, the claim to knowledge that the authors are making. It should indicate the boundaries of space and time within which the enquiry has occurred. If there is a claim to generality beyond the boundaries of the enquiry the basis of that claim should be given, for example that a random sample is thought to be representative of a larger population. There should also be a hint of the method of enquiry

The boundaries of an enquiry are important - and are unfortunately too often omitted from abstracts. This is due to the regrettable tendency for researchers to generalise their results from, for example, a few schools to all schools, and to imply that what was true at a particular time, is true for all time. Some reference to the geographical location of the children, or teachers, or schools on whom the claim to knowledge rests should be made. Because of the international nature of the research community it is worth making clear in what country the research took place. Also the period in which the data was collected should be stated. Chapter Six discusses this matter more fully.

The abstract should be a condensation of the substance of the paper, not a trailer, nor an introduction. Journals and thesis regulations usually put a limit of around 200 to 300 words to the length of an abstract. 'Trailer' is a term borrowed from the cinema industry to describe a showing of a few highlights in order to win an audience. An 'Introduction' tells that something is coming, but doesn't reveal its substance. These are not what is needed.

Abstracts are recycled in abstract journals and electronic networks and provide the main vehicle for other researchers to become aware of particular studies. Hence the more clearly they convey the claim to knowledge of the original paper the more useful they are in helping the reader to decide whether it is worth taking the trouble to obtain and read the original and possibly cite it in his/her own writing.

Both the abstract and the paper should make sense without the other.

What is a CLAIM TO KNOWLEDGE ?

In research in educational settings a claim to knowledge is likely to be about some theoretical aspect of teaching and learning, or about educational policy, or about teaching or managerial practice. It may, for example:
- contribute incrementally to the accumulated knowledge of the topic under study;
- challenge existing theoretical ideas;
- offer significant improvements to existing practice;
- give new insights into policy;
- introduce a new methodology of potential power;
- provide a 'significant piece in a jigsaw of understanding'; or
- bring together disparate findings and integrate them into a new theoretical structure.

What goes in the INTRODUCTION ?

Having read title, name of author(s), and introduction the reader should know at least the 'what, who, where, when, and why' of the paper. These are:
- what the enquiry was about;
- who is writing about it;

- where the enquiry took place;
- when it happened; and
- why it happened and why an account of it is being published.

'What the enquiry was about' isn't the claim to knowledge of the paper, but is a general statement indicating the field of enquiry, for example 'This is a study of twelve-year old children doing mathematics homework ...'.

'Who is writing about it' is a short statement that puts some flesh and bones to the author's name. For example, '... carried out by myself. I was the children's mathematics teacher and at the time had been teaching in the same school for ten years.' This alerts the reader to potential advantages and disadvantages that the author may have had in conducting the research. Contrast it with 'I was a visitor to the school and initially the children did not know me.' These statements alert the reader to the possibility that the relationship, or lack of relationship, between the researcher and children may have a bearing on the outcome of the enquiry, and so enable the reader to examine the paper critically to see whether the researcher has recognised the implications of this. Positivist researchers tend to believe that the researcher is not a variable of any consequence, but researchers working within the interpretative paradigm know that this may not be true.

'Where the enquiry took place' entails either a specific description, eg 'The enquiry took place at Millfield Comprehensive School in Barsetshire, England' or if it is important to preserve anonymity '... at a rural comprehensive school in an English county.' Again this alerts the reader's critical faculties. In my view the specific description is best because it stresses the singular nature of the enquiry, whereas the latter description may lead the reader into fallacious thoughts about rural, or comprehensive or county schools in general.

'When it happened'. Anyone who has experienced the rapid changes in the curriculum in, for example, English schools over the last few years will recognise the importance of putting a date to enquiries.

'Why the enquiry happened and why an account of it is being published'. The first question gives the reader insight into the spark of excitement that triggered off the enquiry, and the second gives a justification for publishing it. This is all part of building up a context for the reader.

Chapter Five ON THE WRITING OF RESEARCH IN EDUCATION

What goes in the CONCEPTUAL BACKGROUND ?

This should set the scene in which the search for a claim to knowledge has been made. It describes the 'state of the art' prior to the claim of the report. It may be in the form of theory-in-the-literature, or common-sense-theory, or both.

If the conceptual background is in the form of theory-in-the-literature, reference to theory in terms of significant studies (carefully cited - see section 7) is required: this may just be a pertinent selection, and if so the rationale for the selection will be helpful to the reader. Accuracy in describing the claims to knowledge of others is important (in my reading of research papers too many authors fail too often in this respect!) There should be a clear logic to the ordering of references and it may be appropriate to make this overt at the beginning. A chronological order is rarely the most satisfactory. Avoidance of what I call genuflection, sandbagging and kingmaking is recommended. These terms are described in section 6. Of course, if a competent review of the literature has recently been published by someone else it may be sufficient just to refer to this.

If the conceptual background is in the form of common-sense-theory, it should be articulated with an indication of the people who are believed to 'own' this common-sense theory.

Consider the following example:
> Most infant teachers hold that play is an important part of educational practice.

In the strictest tradition, where every assertion is supported by a reference to the literature, it would be necessary to pin to the end of this the name of some author who has demonstrated that this is the case. Suppose I can't find one, yet have no doubt of the veracity of my statement. What do I do? I could omit it, but this might damage the logic of my writing. I could waste a lot of time hunting for a suitable reference. But why not write it like this, treating it as a common-sense utterance that I expect to be believed by all who read the paper:
> I believe that most infant teachers hold that play is an important part of educational practice.

This directly attributes the assertion to an individual, myself, and as such could be seen as a rigorous locating of the assertion, although it adds nothing to the evidence for making such a statement.

Perhaps the most important guideline for deciding when the citing of unreferenced common-sense knowledge is appropriate, is the question 'Does the claim to knowledge I am making depend upon it?' If it does then the starting point must be substantiated.

In my view too little attention has been paid to the epistemology of the writing of conceptual backgrounds of academic papers. For example, too often statements of belief like the above get subsequently quoted as though they were statements of fact by virtue of a bolted-on reference, eg:

> Most infant teachers hold that play is an important part of educational practice (Bassey 1993).

What goes in the METHOD OF ENQUIRY ?

This section should describe how the data were collected. If someone else's method was used, or adapted, the source should be cited. A rationale for the chosen method, and for the rejection of alternatives, may be appropriate, if there is sufficient space.

Ideally, sufficient detail should be given so that others could replicate the research. If this would be too demanding of the available space then at least enough of the method should be described for the reader to be able to evaluate the enquiry and have an idea of the credibility of the claim to knowledge in relation to the method used

A reference to the ethical stance may be appropriate.

What goes in the DATA COLLECTION ?

This section should indicate the extent of raw data obtained, including the boundary of space and time within which it was collected. The purpose is to give sufficient evidence for the reader to decide whether the data obtained by the researcher are appropriate for the purpose, whether sufficient data have been collected, and whether the researchers have maintained their ethical stance. Providing a table of raw data, or giving an example of a interview transcript or an observation report, may help the reader to get a feeling of the credibility of the research.

This section often merges with the next.

What goes in the DATA ANALYSIS AND INTERPRETATION ?

This should describe how the data was analysed and interpreted in order to make the claim to knowledge. The aim should be to provide a sufficient account for the reader to judge the validity of the analysis. This section may link up with the Conceptual Background, by showing how the findings of other mesh into the present work and contribute to the new claim to knowledge.

Often tables or diagrams are helpful here. The content of tables should be restricted to data that are essential to the analysis. Within tables there should be a rationale for the order of the items, and an explanation of this in a footnote to the table. Calculated numbers should not be given to greater accuracy than the raw data merits. Columns and rows of data should be labelled in ways that make sense to the reader without needing to re-read the text.

Diagrams are a pictorial way of representing the analysis and giving a visual condensation of the argument. It is worth testing drafts of diagrams on critical friends to ensure that they are meaningful and helpful to potential readers. In charts, like tables, it is important to have a rationale for the order of items that can be explained in a footnote.

Both tables and diagrams deserve titles that are self-explanatory.

What goes in the EMPIRICAL CONCLUSION ?

The Empirical Conclusion should express the claim to knowledge that arises from the analysis and interpretation of the data. It should be a claim within the boundary of the enquiry: extrapolation beyond this boundary, if appropriate, should be reserved for the next section. The Empirical Conclusion will probably be a longer statement than that in the Abstract but because I recommend that it is strictly focused on the logical outcome of the data of the research, it is likely to be a brief section of the paper. It may use exactly the same words as appear in the Abstract.

The rationale for emphasising *Empirical* Conclusion is further discussed in Chapter Seven.

What goes in REFLECTIONS or DISCUSSION or GENERAL CONCLUSION?

This section will probably link the Empirical Conclusion with the Conceptual Background in order to show how the present claim to knowledge fits in with previous knowledge. Some authors prefer to call this 'Discussion'.

It may include reflective comment on the more general implications of the claim to knowledge for classroom practice, or educational policy. It is here that the authors may feel able to suggest that the results can be extrapolated beyond the boundaries of the enquiry, ie 'what we found in our setting may also occur in other similar settings'. If this is a strong feature of the paper perhaps this section should be called 'General Conclusion'.

This section may also give comments on ways in which the methodology could be improved or on the implications for further research.

What about the TITLE ?

In my view devising the title is the very last stage of writing a paper. Only at the end is a writer sure what the paper is about!

It should convey the claim to knowledge and the boundary in which it arises. In effect the title should be a summary of the Abstract! For example:
> Sharp pencils improve handwriting in three Nottinghamshire infant schools.

This gives the claim to knowledge and tells that the boundary within which that claim is being made was quite limited. It is, of course, a more honest title than:
> Sharp pencils improve handwriting.

Some writers try to create witty titles, for example:
> Sharp swords give glittering proses.

This title may be eye-catching in a magazine or newspaper, but is unlikely to make any impact in a research journal, for others working in the field of handwriting improvement are unlikely to recognise its relevance. If the author is so enamoured of the parody of FE Smith's aphorism, the double title approach could be adopted, eg
> Sharp swords give glittering proses: pencils and handwriting in some infant schools

However, editors can get stroppy about the length of titles.

What about the REFERENCES?

The Harvard system is widely used in educational research journals and is the one I recommend to my students. The educational literature is complicated, and the techniques for citing from articles in journals, articles in texts, articles in edited texts, paragraphs in government papers, etc. take time to master. Section 7 gives an account of this system.

6. SOME FLAWS AND FRIPPERIES IN RESEARCH PAPERS

This is a personal list of what I see as 'flaws and fripperies' in research papers. Perhaps my criticisms are not widely shared in the research community, for I find many instances of them!

The examples are invented.

(a)   ... in general

UNCERTAIN CLAIM TO KNOWLEDGE   Failing to make clear what is the claim to knowledge of the report. The claim should be in both the abstract and the main text and should make clear what is the boundary (in space and time) to the claim.

OPAQUENESS   Writing in a way that is not readily understood by most potential readers. This may be due to a complex literary style, to unusual vocabulary, or to lack of progression in argument, etc. It is writing that gets the research 'off the author's chest' but not 'into the minds' of the readers.

WORDINESS   Writing at greater length than is necessary to convey the required meaning.

(b)   ... in the conceptual background

GENUFLECTION   Ritualistic citing of the founding parents of theory.

SANDBAGGING   Adding to a statement inert defences to make it look secure.

KINGMAKING   Giving undue authority to somebody by citing unresearched utterances.

For example:

Piaget (1926) showed that children develop in stages and so it is no surprise to find that libraries for children are usually organised according to levels of complexity for readers (Adams 1980, Brown 1982, Collins 1988). In planning this investigation we started with the view stated by Davidson (1981, p1) that any collection of writings is a library. In designing our questionnaire, we used a modified form of that used by Edwards (1987) ...

The reference to the work of Piaget is genuflection, to that of Adams, Brown, and Collins, sandbagging, and to that of Davidson kingmaking. These add little to the account but make the reference list look impressive. They are unnecessary. The reference to Edwards is, of course, essential: its absence would amount to plagiarism.

(c)   ... in the description of data

HIDING THE INSTRUMENTS   Not making clear what questions were asked or what behaviours were observed.

For example:

Seventy per cent of the sample were not happy with the school rule banning the wearing of jeans.
(No evidence of what the question asked was).

WRITING IN LOCAL JARGON   Using the in-house jargon of the researchers instead of translating it into readily understood language.

For example:

Of the NH respondents to the BWJ rule ...
(Meaning the 'Not Happy' respondents to the 'Banning the Wearing of Jeans' rule).

(d)   ... in the analysis of data

OVER-CRUNCHING NUMBERS   Giving a numerical result to greater accuracy than that of the raw data. For example:

Child	No. of times child off-task	Period of observation	No. of times off-task per 10 min.
Child 1	5	10 min	5
Child 2	7	12 min	5.83

NOT STATISTICALLY SIGNIFICANT BUT...   Then why mention it?

For example:

More of the older group than of the younger group agreed with the statement, but the difference was not statistically significant.

This error I find to be widespread. It is as though the researcher, having spent hours on number crunching that led to a conclusion that the numerical differences found were not statistically significant, is either determined to get some credit for the work done, or doesn't trust the statistical test!

(e)   ... in stating conclusions

SUPPRESSION OF MINORITIES   Commending a practice where the research result shows that this has been of benefit to a majority - but not to a minority - of participants.

For example:

This research involved a random sample of schools informing parents of the LEA truancy policy. It was found that in 50% of the schools truancy was reduced during the next term, in 30% there was no difference, and in 20% it increased. It is concluded that sending this information regularly to parents is advantageous.

On the face of it, even if the sample was truly representative and a causal link between the information and the incidence of truancy has been established, the conclusion will be accurate in half of the cases and false in the other half.

OVER-GENERALISING   Generalising from the results of research on an opportunity sample to a whole population.

For example:

This study was conducted in three infant schools in Nottingham. ... The results show that pupils write more clearly when schools issue them with sharp pencils.

7. REFERENCING SYSTEMATICALLY

One of the few aspects of research about which there is unanimity among the research community is that in the writing of academic papers there are strict procedures for ensuring that each reference to the writing of others is effectively documented. This is something that we need to ensure is firmly established in the minds of those whom we train in research.

Most academic writing relates to some extent to work carried out by others and it is expected that these links will be made clear. Indeed, not to do this is to leave oneself open to the serious charge of plagiarism. Plagiarism is usually defined as the presenting of the work of others as though it were one's own. Reproducing the words of another without acknowledging the source is an extreme form of plagiarism, but to rewrite a detailed account or argument without acknowledgement of its original author is also unacceptable to the academic community. The procedures described here are designed to avoid plagiarism and to ensure that an interested reader can check back to the original document with the minimum of difficulty.

'Citation' I take to mean the mention of an author's work in the text of an academic journal. The method I recommend to my students is the 'Harvard' system . There are, of course, other ways of handling references, but experience suggests that this is the most useful method for students writing long essays, dissertations and theses, as it is for academics writing books and papers. The system used in earlier writings, that involved Latin phrases such as 'ibid', 'idem' and 'op cit' tends to be clumsy.

References

At the end of the academic paper the references are given, under the heading of 'References', as an alphabetical list of documents cited, expressed in a number of forms. This list shows the conventions used in the British Educational Research Journal.

> BALL, S. J. (1990) *Politics and Policy Making in Education* (London, Routledge)
>
> DEPARTMENT OF EDUCATION AND SCIENCE (1989a) *From Policy to Practice* (London, HMSO)
>
> DEPARTMENT OF EDUCATION AND SCIENCE (1989b) *The Education Reform Act 1988: the School Curriculum and Assessment* (London, HMSO)
>
> GRIFFITHS, M. & DAVIES, C. (1993) Learning to learn: action research from an equal opportunities perspective in a junior school, *British Educational Research Journal,* 19(1) pp. 43-58
>
> PETERSON, P.L., FENNEMA, E. & CARPENTER, T.P. (1991) Teachers' knowledge of students' mathematics problem solving knowledge, in: J.E.BROPHY (Ed.) *Advances in Research on Teaching Vol 2: Teachers' Subject Matter Knowledge* (Greenwich, CY, JAI Press)

The surname is given first, in capitals, followed by a comma and then the author's initials, with stops. If there are several names they are all listed, with commas between and the last being preceded by an ampersand. First names are not given, only initials. Next comes the year of publication, in brackets. If more than one reference cited in the writing was published by the author in that year, the form is (1989a), (1989b) etc. If the reference is to a book, as in the Ball example, the title is given in lower case with appropriate initial letters in capitals; the whole title is in italics (or underlined if italic print is not available). If the reference is to a paper in a journal, as in the Griffiths and Davies example, the title of the paper is given in lower case and then the title of the journal is given in the same way as the title of a book - in italics or underlined. Immediately after the title of a book the publisher's name is given, in brackets, and preceded by the place of publication. Immediately after the name of a journal there is a comma, followed by the volume number and, if there is a part to the volume, as is usually the case, this is given in brackets immediately following the volume number; next the abbreviation 'pp' is used to refer to page numbers and then the number of the first and last pages of the article in the journal are given.

In principle it is simple, in detail complicated, but it is very systematic. It is more easily learned through example than by rule.

Practice among publishers varies slightly and there is no need for any of us to be neurotic about the use and positions of commas and stops in these lists, although being systematic throughout a list is obviously sensible, since lack of it can irritate any readers who are fastidious in these matters. The essence of the Harvard system is that, notwithstanding the above detail, it is a relatively simple system to use. Once a paper has been put in the reference list, it can be cited as often as necessary without much further fuss.

Citation

In the text the citation is given in terms of the author's surname with the year date in brackets. For example:

>Ball (1990) identified a number of different ideological positions taken by conservative politicians.

This is a general comment on his book. But if a precise reference, such as a quotation, is used, it is correct to give the page reference, thus:

>Ball (1990, p9) refers to 'the messy realities' in the educational policy process.

A longer quotation would normally be inset (ie wider margins, possibly smaller print) in the writer's text and then it is more usual to put the page number at the end of the quotation.

>Ball (1990) refers to:
>
>>'the messy realities of influence, pressure, dogma, expediency, conflict, compromise, intransigence, resistance, error, opposition and pragmatism in the policy process'. (p9)

Numbered notes

In addition to the citation and reference system sometimes it is helpful to use a number sequence for notes. These are either listed at the end of the paper, or given as footnotes at the bottom of pages. The idea of a note is something that may contribute to the reader's understanding of the text, but that would unnecessarily interfere with the flow of the text if inserted in the middle of it. For example:

>(1) Discussion of this idea with Dr A Brown has helped me to clarify this issue.
>
>(2) The definition of 'informal' used here has been chosen because it is felt that on the one hand...

On examining the original

It is expected that every referenced item listed has been examined by the writer in the original (either in the journal or book, as a reprint sent by the author, or as a photocopy obtained from a library) in order to avoid the possibility of the errors of one abstracter being repeated by the next, but where this proves impossible the item should carry an indication of where the paper has been cited. For example:

> ATKINS, M.J. (1982) *Foundation Courses in a Sixth Form College: a Case Study*, unpublished PhD thesis, University of Nottingham. Cited in Ball (1990)

The Ball reference is then listed in its alphabetical position.

Delineating a literature search

How many references should be cited in an academic paper? There are two obvious outer limits: the number of relevant references that exist and the time available for searching for them, reading and digesting them, and expressing the essence of their content. On a taught course, say for an MEd, there is only a limited amount of time available for library work, because of other demands of the course. On a master's research degree, say MPhil or MA, there is more time and a student may be expected to cover more of the literature. On a doctorate study, as with an academic paper, there is usually an expectation that an exhaustive review of relevant literature will have been made.

Inevitably it is a matter of circumstances and individual judgement as to how many references should be consulted, and, of those consulted, how many should be cited. But I find this guideline for procedure useful. Be systematic in both the search and in recording how the search was made. For example, a note (using the number system suggested above) in this form makes relevant details of the search clear to the reader:

> (1) In preparing this literature review British Education Abstracts was searched from January 1980 to December 1993. Of 52 papers referring to problem solving in primary school mathematics it was judged from the abstracts that 14 were pertinent to this enquiry. Twelve are cited in Chapter One; the following two papers were, unfortunately, unobtainable: ... For work carried out prior to 1980 I have relied on the review article by Smith and Robinson (1982).

8. ON WRITING REFLECTIVE RESEARCH PAPERS IN EDUCATION

In Chapter One reflective research is described as systematic and critical thinking in which the findings of empirical research are the starting point for critical review and logical argument. In what form are the outcomes of this research communicated?

This kind of writing is less easy to formalise than the writing of the results of empirical research, but empirical and reflective writing have a key element in common. They are both about making a claim to knowledge. Thus empirical assertions need to be based on cited evidence, or on logical constructions from cited evidence. Value statements need to be attributed to their proponents and should exhibit a coherence of belief. Analytical processes need to be explained in terms of a rationale for using them. If new theoretical constructs are proposed they need to be justified. If recommendations for policy or practice are proposed they need to arise clearly from the discussion and analysis of evidence and articulated belief.

At the time of writing (December 1993) the Report of the National Commission on Education has just been published. It is an example of reflective writing at its best, in that: (a) it starts with a clear statement of the shared beliefs of its authors; (b) it is firmly ground in evidence that is extensively cited; and (c) from careful analysis of this evidence it leads to clearly enunciated and attributed recommendations. This is illustrated in Figure [7].

Figure [7]   Extracts from the report of the National Commission on Education (1993)* that illustrate good reflective writing

(a) 'a clear statement of shared beliefs of its authors'

The Commission's vision ... In the United Kingdom much higher achievement in education and training is needed to match world standards ... All children must achieve a good grasp of literacy and basic skills early on as the foundation for learning throughout life ... It it is the role of education *both* to interpret and pass on the values of society *and* to stimulate people to think for themselves and to change the world around them. (p43)

(b) 'firmly ground in evidence'

A large-scale study that examined the relationship between children's pre-school experiences and their attainment at 5 and 10 years of age reported marked differences in ability, attainment and behaviour at age 10 between those who had attended pre-school groups and those who had not. (Osborn, A.F. and Milbank, J.E., 1987. *The Effects of Early Education: a Report from the Child Health and Education Study*. Oxford University Press) (p 114)

(c) 'clearly enunciated and attributed recommendations'

This leads us to recommend a national strategy for improving early childhood education and care. A major component should be a statutory requirement on local authorities to ensure that sufficient high-quality, publicly-funded nursery education places are available for all 3- and 4-year-olds whose parents wish it. (pp131-132)

**Learning to Succeed*, report of the National Commission on Education (1993), London, Heinemann

In some ways the concept of a reflective paper is like that of an empirical paper (see Figure [6]) but without the sections entitled 'Method of enquiry' and 'Data collection', and with the sections called 'Conceptual background', 'Data analysis and interpretation', 'Conclusion' and 'Reflections' all run together and redivided into sections that represent the logic of the particular paper. In other words most of the ideas about writing expressed earlier in this chapter apply equally to reflective writing.

9. WRITING FOR THE READER LUCIDLY AND COGENTLY

How does one learn to write more effectively? Getting a 'critical friend' to comment on one's style as well as on one's ideas can be valuable, but demands time of the friend. The most important critic is likely to be the self. For example, Tolkein, writing about criticisms of his writing in the foreword to *The Lord of the Rings* (1966 edition) refers to himself as 'the most critical reader of all.' Putting each draft of a paper on one side for a few days and then trying to read it as audience rather than as writer, can be helpful. Personally I aim to subject my writing sentence by sentence, and paragraph by paragraph, to a merciless scrutiny for correctness, lucidity and cogency - but I know that I still fail sometimes in getting my meaning across.

A reference book I would not be without is H.W.Fowler's (1926) *A Dictionary of Modern English Usage* . Mine is the second edition, revised in 1965 by Sir Ernest Gower, who writes in its preface:

> What is the secret of its success? It is not that all Fowler's opinions are unchallengeable. Many have been challenged. It is not that he is always easy reading. At his best he is incomparable. But he never forgot what he calls 'that pestilent fellow the critical reader' who is 'not satisfied with catching the general drift and obvious intention of a sentence' but insists that 'the words used must ... actually yield on scrutiny the desired sense'. (p iii)

Likewise I make regular use of the *Concise Oxford Dictionary* to check the meanings of words that I doubt - and the wordprocessor spellcheck to remove most of my typographic errors.

It seems that many of the people formally educated in the 1960s onwards were inadequately trained in punctuation, spelling and grammar. A recent Open University text by Collinson, Kirkup, Kyd and Slocombe (1992) called *Plain English* can be helpful. It provides self-tests and exercises on punctuation, spelling, grammar, and style, and was written 'to meet the needs of all students who wish to improve their writing skills'.

Chapter Five ON THE WRITING OF RESEARCH IN EDUCATION

Some word processor programmes now include quite sophisticated grammar checks, although the use of these can take a lot of time. I recommend them to those students who don't seem to recognise that sentences need verbs ...!

* * * * *

This has not been an easy chapter to write for, in the back of my mind has been a piece of doggerel of whose author I have lost track.

> *Teach not thy parent's mother*
> *The juices of the egg to take by suction,*
> *For sure she can that feat enact*
> *Without the aid of thy instruction.*

At the same time I sense that researchers in education, as an academic community, are stronger on enquiry than on scholarship; better at asking questions than at writing up the answers.

Learning to write well is a never-ending art.

Chapter Six

ON SEARCH FOR GENERALISATIONS

Sections

1.	THE TRADITIONAL EXPECTATION THAT EDUCATIONAL RESEARCH SHOULD PROVIDE GENERALISATIONS WHICH COULD BE USEFUL TO TEACHERS	88
2.	THREE ARGUMENTS TO SUPPORT THE CLAIM THAT THERE ARE FEW GENERALISATIONS OF USE TO TEACHERS	89
3.	OPEN AND CLOSED GENERALISATIONS	97
4.	EXAMPLES OF STATEMENTS MADE AS OPEN GENERALISATIONS THAT SHOULD HAVE BEEN EXPRESSED AS CLOSED GENERALISATIONS	100
5.	THE VALUE OF GENERALISATIONS FOR POLICY-MAKERS	103

Chapter Six   ON SEARCH FOR GENERALISATIONS

One day I heard a nine-year-old girl, who was watching her two-year-old brother, say to her mother, 'Mum. You know your willy. Well, he's playing with his.' Psychoanalysts might make something of generalising the genitals, but to me it was just an instance of the way in which we all try to generalise from one to all, and this starts at an early age. Charles Darwin's son is said to have asked a friend where his father studied his whelks. We all - children and adults alike - tend to extrapolate from our experience to expect elsewhere to be the same. It must be a cognitive device for conserving memory space, for without it there would be so much more to remember.

Unfortunately, some researchers expect the same from their research findings. In 1981 I wrote a paper for the *Oxford Review of Education* entitled 'Pedagogic research: on the relative merits of search for generalisation and study of single events'. I was trying to establish that British researchers at that time seemed to more or less concur on two points: (a) that educational research should result in generalisations which could coalesce into educational theory, and (b) that educational research should contribute in some way to the improvement of educational practice. My purpose was to support the worthwhileness of the second point but to attack the viability of the first.

Since then the belief in the potential power of generalisation has waned, encouraged by books such as that edited by Simons (1980), *Towards a Science of the Singular,* and by the rise of the action research movement in schools. Keeves (1988) in his editorial introduction to *Educational Research, Methodology, and Measurement: an International Handbook,* said:

> There was a blooming of educational research activity during the 1960s and 1970s, with much research being carried out within the scientific approach. This peak in activity was relatively short-lived. ... it is now widely recognised that the scientific or positivistic approach, while highly successful in many areas of inquiry, cannot take into account all the many aspects of human behaviour and the influences of the social context on that behaviour. (pp3-4)

Nevertheless there remain many critics of educational research who, taking a scientific perspective, fail to understand the unlikelihood of finding useful generalisations and who denigrate studies of singularities. [The House of Lords speech by Lord Skidelsky reported in Chapter Three is a case in point]. Hence it is important to keep the arguments alive. The following section reproduces and extends arguments which I put in my 1981 paper to substantiate the view that there are few generalisations about education which are of value to teachers. I have not changed my mind.

1. THE TRADITIONAL EXPECTATION THAT EDUCATIONAL RESEARCH SHOULD PROVIDE GENERALISATIONS WHICH COULD BE USEFUL TO TEACHERS

Eggleston (1979), giving the presidential address to the British Educational Research Association in 1978, set out to 'map the domain' of educational research. He suggested how 'descriptions of schooling ... could be generalised'. He said:

> We are still ignorant of the strategies teachers use such as the selection of facts to be taught, the experiences given to pupils to advance concept development or to train them in specified skills. We do not know how teachers sequence experiences, design and use diagnostic procedures and instruments to monitor pupils' progress, of the strategies they use to maintain motivation or other conditions for learning or even to make the classroom a congenial place to be.

Stones (1979), in his textbook *Psychopedagogy,* in which he linked psychological knowledge of learning with professional ideas about teaching, said:

> although teachers are undoubtedly different, there is an important basic core of sameness which does enable us ... to make some generalizations about the nature of teaching.

He expected that the joint activity of teachers and researchers would lead to 'a theory of teaching' which would entail 'new regularities in the form of theoretical principles'.

Cohen and Manion (1980) in *Research Methods in Education,* which became a popular resource text in the 1980s, put particular stress on scientific methods of enquiry, and indicated that 'the ultimate aim of science is theory.' They saw the scientist as concerned 'to generalise his findings to the world at large', although they recognised that the human scientist, including the educational researcher, has 'to exercise great caution when generalising his findings.'

Nisbet, six years before this publication, in an address to the inaugural meeting of the British Educational Research Association, had expressed a contrary view (1974) to that of educational science and problem solving.

> I think that recent years have seen a move away from the naive idea that problems are solved by educational research: that is the old 'Educational Science' idea, and it is a myth. Educational research can strengthen the information base of decision-making; its procedures of inquiry and evaluation can inject rigour ... investigation into teaching and learning sharpens thinking, directs attention to important issues, clarifies problems, encourages debate and the exchange of views, and thus deepens understanding. ... Research of this kind aims to increase the problem-solving capacity of the educational system, rather than to provide the final answers to questions.

Stenhouse (1980) cut through this discussion with the profound assertion that

Chapter Six   ON SEARCH FOR GENERALISATIONS

> the most important distinction in educational research at this moment is that between the study of samples and the study of cases.

Linking his 1980 paper with one written in 1978 it is clear that he expected both the study of samples and the study of cases to lead to generalisations. He distinguished between *predictive generalisations*, which arise from the study of samples and are the form in which data are accumulated in science, and *retrospective generalisations*, which can arise from the analysis of case-studies and are the form in which data are accumulated in history. He wrote:

> while predictive generalisations claim to supersede the need for individual judgement, retrospective generalisations seek to strengthen individual judgement where it cannot be superseded.

In this book I use the single word 'generalisation' for his 'predictive generalisation' because to me the essential value of a generalisation is that it can be used to predict events. I am less certain about Stenhouse's use of the term 'retrospective generalisation'. To me the value of the findings of a study of a singularity lies in the extent to which someone can *relate* their own experience to the singularity and so learn from it. This is examined in the next chapter.

2. THREE ARGUMENTS TO SUPPORT THE CLAIM THAT THERE ARE FEW GENERALISATIONS OF USE TO TEACHERS

(a)   Evidence from Maccoby and Jacklin (1974) *The Psychology of Sex Differences*

A large volume of research has been conducted on the possibility of differences occurring between the classroom performance of boys and girls. Maccoby and Jacklin (1974) reviewed 1400 studies in this field and identified only four statements about sex differences in performance and behaviour of children and young people which they considered to be 'fairly well established'. These are:

- that teenage girls have greater verbal ability,
- that adolescent boys have greater mathematical ability,
- that adolescent boys excel in visual-spatial ability, and
- that males at all ages are more aggressive than females.

The first three of these statements are based on a number of studies where tests have been used and which enable the statements to be quantified. The differences vary slightly from one investigation to another, but overall the emerging pattern is of differences amounting to about one-third of a standard deviation.

Even if a class contained the same distribution of ability between girls and boys as large-scale samples, the differences are so slight that they could not provide useful pedagogic knowledge to teachers. Teachers seeking to know about the verbal, visual-spatial, and general mathematical abilities of their pupils, need to study the pupils, not inapplicable generalisations.

Regrettably these generalisations are widely known: they have probably done harm, for this reason. They arise from studies of large populations. When applied to small populations such as classes of say 30 children, the differences in ability between girls and boys will not necessarily mirror the findings from large populations. For example, in classes of 15 boys and 15 girls the average verbal ability of the girls will sometimes be greater than the average for the boys, sometimes be equal, and sometimes be less. But if the teachers expect the girls to be of greater verbal ability than the boys, the way they plan and conduct their lessons may well enhance the verbal ability of the girls relative to the boys, thus fulfilling the expectation.

I argue that these four generalisations, arising from 1400 research studies, are not useful to teachers.

In general it must be the case that any research investigation which is based on large samples of children (in order to give confidence to its conclusions) and which detects differences in the average abilities of sub-sets of the whole, is not going to provide useful predictive information for the individual teacher working with similar sub-sets in a class of about 30 children. The value of such an investigation lies only in drawing attention to the existence of differences in the sub-sets of large populations, and thus alerting teachers to the value of personally observing and testing each individual child in order to teach each child effectively.

(b) Evidence from Entwistle and Nisbet (1972) *Educational Research in Action*

In 1972 Entwistle and Nisbet published a companion volume to their methodological text *Educational Research Methods* (1970) and called it *Educational Research in Action*. Their aim was to give examples of 'empirical studies which are intrinsically interesting and which illustrate important research strategies'. This book gives a valuable insight into the kinds of educational research which were significant in Britain around 1970.

A large section of it is devoted to 28 extracts from research papers in education published mainly between 1966 and 1972. I carefully considered these 28 extracts and decided that 15 of them contained empirical generalisations by way of conclusions. The other extracts were descriptive accounts of various research and teaching methods. The 15 are listed below, with

Chapter Six ON SEARCH FOR GENERALISATIONS

my brief synopsis and my evaluation in response to the question: could the generalisation(s) be useful to teachers who are trying to improve their teaching?

Barnes D (1969) 'Language, the learner and the school'

Synopsis — This is a study of the language used in twelve lessons in the first term of entry to secondary school. Barnes explains that his original conception of the research was 'that generalisation drawn from a few secondary lessons could be put beside others drawn from primary school, and light thrown on some difficulties of adjustment faced by new entries to secondary schools'. At the end of a detailed analysis of parts of these lessons, he concludes that he has 'a basis for arguing (a) that some teachers fail to perceive the pedagogical implications of many of their own uses of language, and (b) that a descriptive study such as this provides a potential method of helping teachers to become more aware.'

Useful to teachers? — Yes, particularly as a starting point for action research into one's own use of language.

Comment — By saying '*some* teachers' and 'a *potential* method' Barnes recognises that these generalisations only apply in certain cases.

Richards P N and Bolton N (1971) 'Types of mathematics teaching, mathematical ability and divergent thinking in junior school children'

Synopsis — From a study of 265 eleven-year-olds in three schools in NE England it was concluded that 'performance on tests of mathematical ability is largely determined by a general ability factor, with the divergent thinking dimension contributing to only certain of the mathematics tests and then to only a very small extent. It is suggested that teaching approaches which foster divergent thinking will, consequently, produce minimal beneficial effects on children's performance on tests of mathematical ability. The results supplied by a comparison of three schools taught by different methods support Biggs' (1967) finding that the use of activity methods in the junior school produces inferior mechanical and problem performance.'

Useful to teachers? — Possibly, if the result is to be believed.

Comment — The generalisations are extrapolations from the findings in only three schools and as such must be suspect. But the paper stimulated debate about the worthwhileness of different kinds of mathematical activity.

Wragg E C (1970) 'Interaction analysis as a feedback system for student teachers'

Synopsis — An account of Flanders' system of interaction analysis and of its value for student teachers in training. 'Flanders has provided strong evidence that students trained in

	Interaction Analysis are better able to control their own classroom behaviour than untrained students.'
Useful to teachers?	Could be for teachers in training.

Britton J N, Martin N C, and Rosen H (1966) 'Multiple marking of English composition'

Synopsis	The GCE 'O' level English composition scripts of 250 representative candidates were marked by several procedures in an attempt to find a marking procedure that would be more reliable than that in current use. The authors conclude: 'in this case marking by individual examiners with very careful briefing and elaborate arrangements for moderation was in fact significantly less reliable than a multiple mark consisting of three rapid impression marks and a mark for mechanical accuracy'.
Useful to teachers?	Not in classroom work, but useful to teachers engaged in public examinations in English.
Comment	I have included this under the heading of 'researches leading to generalisations' but the actual form of words shows that the researchers were wary of this, for they say 'in this case'.

Fraser E D (1969) Home environment and the school

Synopsis	This study of 408 children in Aberdeen led to the conclusion that 'a normal home background, emotional stability, freedom from tension and from economic insecurity, and consistent encouragement from parents are necessary for a child if his schoolwork is to reach the level allowed by his intelligence'.
Useful to teachers?	No. The teacher has no control over home variables.
Comment.	The phrase 'are necessary' is too absolute. Evidence of the home background of Beethoven, Churchill or Mao Tse Tung is sufficient to falsify this generalisation. It could have been expressed as 'are in many cases necessary'.

Peaker G F (1967) 'The regression analyses of the national survey' (for the Plowden report)

Synopsis	Children's progress in primary school is more influenced by variation in parental attitudes than by variation in home circumstances, and more by the latter than by variations between schools and teachers.
Useful to teachers?	Of no use in the classroom since the teacher has no control over home variables.
Comment	This refers to large populations and not to individual children.

Douglas J W B, Ross J M and Simpson H R (1968) 'All our future'

Synopsis	A report from a longitudinal and cross-sectional study of 5362 people born in Great Britain in the first week of March 1946. At this stage the sample is reported on at

Chapter Six   ON SEARCH FOR GENERALISATIONS

	the age of sixteen. A vast amount of data is given concerning social class and performance, attitudes, etc.
Useful to teachers?	Of no use in the classroom.
Comment	The generalisations apply to large populations, not necessarily to small ones, and certainly not to all individuals. This report and the previous one featured significantly in the education studies of many teachers in training and tended to be simplified into the erroneous and horrific view that all working class children had limited educational horizons.

Barker Lunn J C (1970)   'Streaming in the primary school'

Synopsis	A study of the progress of 5500 children in 36 streamed and 36 non-streamed junior schools. It was concluded that 'if one is to judge the streaming/non-streaming issue solely on the basis of academic performance, the findings of this study lend small support to either side'.
Useful to teachers?	No. For the individual teacher the findings were not helpful in the classroom.
Comment	At the time it promoted much debate and as such probably contributed to the destreaming of many schools.

Barker Lunn (1970)   'Attitudes of pupils'

Synopsis	This was part of the previous item and showed some differences between the average attitudes of pupils in non-streamed and streamed classes.
Useful to teachers?	No.
Comment	See above.

Morton-Williams R and French S (1968)   'Schools Council Enquiry 1 - young school leavers'

Synopsis	A study of 4825 pupils and ex-pupils aged between 13 and 16 years. '15 year-old leavers differed most of all from those staying on at school in the quality of their home backgrounds which were much less favourable for leavers, in being very much less inclined to have any intellectual or academic interests, and in being much more interested in practical-construction activities than were stayers.'
Useful to teachers?	No.
Comment	Teachers see this kind of research as telling them what they already know.

Hasan P and Butcher H J (1966)   'Creativity and intelligence'

Synopsis	This investigation was a partial replication of Getzel's and Jackson's study of creativity and intelligence, carried out on 175 Scottish secondary children in the

second year. Much more overlap between creativity and intelligence was found than in the original study.

Useful to teachers? No.

Vernon P E (1971) 'Effects of administration and scoring on divergent thinking tests'

Synopsis Vernon reviewed a number of papers and concluded that 'there is evidence that the conditions of testing, the wording of instructions, and the subjects understanding of what is required, affect the responses in some way'. From his own work with 400 fourteen-year-old Canadians he suggested 'that divergent test scores obtained under relaxed conditions have generally richer psychological meaning than those obtained under more formal, test-like conditions.'

Useful to teachers? No.

Comment Most would say this is obvious.

Nisbet J D and Welsh J (1972) A local evaluation of primary school French

Synopsis This was a study of nearly 2000 secondary school children in Aberdeen. 'The results suggest that primary school French confers some initial advantage, but this advantage diminishes and disappears during the first two secondary years ... If generalisation is permissible from this limited study, the conclusion would appear to be that one should not expect primary school French to confer a lasting advantage, but that justification for the inclusion of French should be within the context of the primary school curriculum in terms of its contribution to the enlargement of interests and understanding and the development of general language skill, rather than its effectiveness as a preparation for secondary work.'

Useful to teachers? No.

Comment May be useful to school governing bodies and local authorities.

Cane B S and Schroeder C (1970) 'The teacher and research'

Synopsis Interviews and postal questionnaires were used to enquire into the research interests and experience of 1060 teachers.

Useful to teachers? No.

Ford J (1969) 'Making friends at school'

Synopsis Sociometric techniques were used to investigate the effect of social class on friendship choices in one comprehensive school, one grammar school and one secondary modern school. The major hypothesis was that 'comprehensive school children will show less tendency to mix with children of their own social type than

Chapter Six ON SEARCH FOR GENERALISATIONS

	will tripartite school children'. The investigator concludes: 'there is no evidence whatever from this study of three schools that this is the case.'
Useful to teachers?	No.
Comment	A major flaw in the hypothesis under test is the assumption that there will be some homogeneity in 'comprehensive school children' and in 'tripartite children'.

In my 1981 paper I wrote: 'much husbandry has resulted in little produce as judged by the criterion of generalisation useful to teachers.' Certainly the examples contained matters of description and discussion which could be of interest to teachers, but there was very little in the way of empirical generalisation which could inform the practice of the individual teacher reading it. On the other hand a number of the studies might be significant for policy making in education.

While the methodological text by Nisbet and Entwistle advocates hypothesis testing in searching for generalisations, their textbook of exemplars suggests that not all research leads to generalisation, but where it does it seems that rarely is the generalisation of use to classroom teachers. I rammed home my point with the following paragraph.

'Perhaps it is significant that at the beginning of their methodological text they give a fictitious generalisation as a basis for discussion of causality:

> We may find that there is a correlation between colour preferences and school attainment. Those children who choose garish colours tend to do badly in exams.

Nisbet and Entwistle use this to illustrate the point that survey data do not establish causality. With the wealth of real research data that they had available, why did they choose a fictitious example? Perhaps this is evidence of the paucity of generalisations which are relevant to classrooms.'

In an earlier version of this paper (Bassey 1980), given to a meeting of the Classroom Action Research Network, I took the example of a generalisation used by Ausubel and Robinson (1971, p64) in their widely read undergraduate text entitled *School learning: an introduction to educational psychology*. It is this:

> Crocodiles eat children.

I said: 'This is a curious statement in that thousands of children visit crocodiles all over the world in zoos every year, and yet reports of them being eaten are very rare. If the statement is to be a generalisation within the meaning of this essay, ie that it predicts future events, it needs to be expressed in a possible and not absolute sense, viz: crocodiles may eat children. The likelihood of a child being eaten depends upon whether the child comes within striking distance of the crocodile's jaws, whether the crocodile senses the child, whether the crocodile is hungry and how quick the child is!'

This bizarre discussion had, of course, a vicious bite, for I concluded it by saying: 'In my view Ausubel and Robinson's example of a generalisation, in their textbook *School learning,* is peculiarly apt. I suspect that every general statement made about school learning has the same property of lack of certainty.'

(c) Evidence from Cohen (1976) *Educational Research in Classrooms and Schools*

Cohen's (1976) text for students provides another approach to the question as to whether research in education provides empirical generalisations which are useful to teachers. The author sets out the purpose of the book as: (a) to introduce the reader to the purpose and techniques of observing pupils and teachers in school and classroom settings; (b) to provide the reader with research tools to assist observations and the systematic recording of data; (c) to develop an understanding of techniques of analysis by way of interpreting observations; (d) to suggest research topics that the reader can undertake; and (e) to introduce relevant empirical studies that help illuminate the suggested topics of research. Over 300 research papers are cited, mainly from British and American journals, and about 120 'research tools' are described in sufficient detail for the reader to use; examples are Maw and Maw's 'Curiosity measures', Dommert's version of the 'Rokeach Dogmatism Scale', Oliver and Butcher's 'Manchester Survey of Opinion Scales about Education', Rutter's Child Behaviour Scale' and McQuitty's 'Linkage Analysis' for identifying staffroom cliques.

Reporting on this book in my 1981 paper, I identified 68 specific suggestions for research investigations in Cohen's book. Of these I considered that 64 are expressed in a form which hints at a hypothesis which could lead to a generalisation. For example:

(a) What is the effect of 'modern' as opposed to 'traditional' methods of mathematics teaching upon junior school children's ability to think divergently? (p27)

(b) Explore the association between classroom climate, teacher values, and teacher pupil contacts and the incidence of curiosity in classroom settings. (p37)

(c) How does class size affect the quality of teaching and learning? (p232)

(d) Study the relationship between personality variables and rigidity in goal-setting behaviour in pupils or college students. (p16)

(e) Do Machiavellian teachers more readily identify Machiavellian pupils? (p72)

(f) What is the difference in the incidence of cheating behaviour in extreme traditional and progressive classroom regimes? (p81)

Chapter Six ON SEARCH FOR GENERALISATIONS

(g) Test the proposition that feelings of superiority are more generally found among those bearing unique names. (p95)

(h) Design a study to explore the relationships between teacher satisfaction, bureaucratic orientation, and school organisation. (p158)

(i) Do teachers hold stereotypic views about the personalities of their pupils from features of their handwriting? (p181)

(j) Test the proposition that headteachers behave differently according to the status of the teacher group with whom they are interacting. (p282)

There are a number of serious methodological issues raised by some of these research proposals - for example matters of ethics, of sample size, and of labelling - but, supposing that it were possible to formulate empirical generalisations from them, how many of these research investigations would help teachers in the business of teaching? Perhaps the first three would be useful, but they would need large scale study which is totally beyond the means of the individual researcher. Yet Cohen describes his list as 'topics which the reader himself can undertake.'

In my view Cohen's book gives further evidence of the scarcity of empirical generalisations which are useful to teachers in their teaching.

3. OPEN AND CLOSED GENERALISATIONS

What is a generalisation? It is an overall statement which brings together a number of individual statements. If a finding arises from the study of one set of events (ie a singularity), then a generalisation is a statement which collates the findings from a number of sets of events (ie several singularities).

It is necessary to distinguish between empirical generalisations which are grounded in facts and logic, and normative generalisations which are grounded in value judgements. Thus statements such as 'the nation needs more engineers' and 'teachers ought to be punctual' are normative generalisations, based on someone's value judgements: they are not empirical generalisations.

I suggest that an important distinction can be made between empirical generalisations which are closed, and those which are open. Let the term 'a closed generalisation' refer to a closed set of events, ie to a set of known events within a defined boundary of space and time. It is a statement which collates findings within a singularity. Let 'an open generalisation' refer to an open set of events, ie to unknown as well as known events. It is a statement which can be extrapolated from the known to the unknown. It follows that while a closed generalisation is descriptive of the known, an open generalisation is both descriptive of the known and predictive of the unknown.

This is an example of a closed generalisation:
> In 1976 a total of 498 Nottinghamshire junior teachers were asked in an interview 'What do you do when your class is in assembly?' Four alternative answers were provided, and many teachers chose more than one. The percentage responses were: attend assembly: 87%; prepare teaching, mark, make displays, etc: 52%; meet with other staff: 32%; work with a small group of remedial children: 16%; no answer: 3%
> Bassey (1978, p53)

This is an example of an open generalisation:
> The great majority of primary school children can only learn efficiently from concrete situations, as lived or described.
> Plowden Report (1967, para 521)

Both statements are empirical generalisations, arising from empirical evidence. The first is 'closed' in space and time because it refers to a particular group of teachers at a particular time. The second is 'open' because it refers to primary school children in general. Both could be seen as useful to teachers in some circumstances. The closed generalisation might be useful to a school where, for example, all of the teachers always attend assemblies, because it might stimulate discussion about the possibility of sometimes using this time more profitably. For schools that already do this, of course the statement is of no consequence. The open generalisation is important to teachers in training as a statement which stresses the value of children working with objects. For experienced teachers, of course, it has become self-evident and assimilated into their personal theories which underpin their classroom practices.

I believe that the opportunities for making open generalisations about educational practice which are truly empirical, are rare. Any requirement that the sample of cases studied should be thoroughly representative of all cases, anywhere in the world and at anytime in the future, is clearly impossible. So when an open generalisation like that of the Plowden Report cited above is made, it comes from a collation of evidence which all encourages the belief that the statement is true. In other words it has the same kind of standing of a law in the natural sciences.

The following statements are open generalisations about the processes of learning.
> The extent to which a person learns something, depends upon factors including:

Chapter Six ON SEARCH FOR GENERALISATIONS

- whether the person is in an affective state conducive to learning (ie whether recent events, the physical context, or the social context act to promote or inhibit positive feelings towards the subject matter);
- whether the person's interest is aroused and maintained (ie whether the subject-matter gives a sense of purpose or challenge in learning it);
- whether the subject-matter is meaningful to the person (ie whether it is clearly communicated to the person and relates to the person's existing knowledge and experience; whether the parts of the subject-matter integrate in the person's mind into a coherent pattern of understanding);
- whether the subject-matter is presented to the person in quantities and at rates which are appropriate for the person; and
- whether the person has opportunities actively to use the new learning and to obtain rapid feed-back on the success of the learning.

These statements can be presumed to be useful to any teacher, today, in the Stone Age and in the twenty-fifth century AD. As such I believe them to be rare.

The arrogance of this assertion that there are few open generalisations of use to teachers is bothersome, because so much educational research has sought to find such. Nevertheless, it seems a succinct way of describing the problem of which many people engaged in educational research are aware. In the paper which I published in 1981 I set out the following quotations to support my case. Nothing that I have read since has altered my view.

Travers (1973) in his editorial introduction to the Second Handbook of Research on Teaching, said:

> In many cases, after reviewing the literature, the author made the decision that the material was such that he could not write a chapter bringing the findings together - the complaint being that the research consisted of a patchwork of unrelated items that neither fitted together nor yielded a useful set of generalisations. (pvii)

Rosenshine and Furst (1973), contributing to the same volume about the use of direct observation to study teaching, said:

> It is possible that the patterns of effective teaching for different ends are so idiosyncratic that they will never be isolated. (p175)

Entwistle (1973), writing for the Open University, said:

> As far as educational research is concerned, the paradigm of the hypothetico-deductive method is an ideal rarely achieved. The complexity of children's behaviour in a classroom often leaves research workers still at the stage of hypothesis hunting. Elaborate theories with accurate prediction lie in the future.

> ... Science provides important guidelines, but here is the uneasy realisation that social science may, after all, be different in kind from natural science.

Beard, Bligh and Harding (1978) in a monograph for the Society for Research into Higher Education on research into teaching methods in higher education came to the following conclusion:

> The growth of educational research [into teaching methods in higher education] has been accompanied in recent years by a growth of criticism of its methods and consequently of its results. There are so many variables that it is impossible to control all of them; even obviously important variables may sometimes remain uncontrollable. In addition, there are unpredictable effects. Human subjects when assigned to experimental and controlled groups differ from the biologists' wheat grains in being autonomous. They may choose to remove themselves, to compare notes with other students who are subjected to a different treatment; or they may resent, or enjoy, a new method that their motivation and performance are significantly affected while it retains its novelty. Fatigue, pressure from other work, or some kind of distraction may also affect results. Even when experiments seem to be conducted successfully, the results usually apply to only certain groups of students. They provide little information about individuals and rarely establish causal relationships and it is often difficult to draw conclusions having general application. ...
>
> While it is true that we seem almost as far as ever from developing a theory of instruction, there is at least a fairly substantial body of information to provide ideas for teachers who wish to try new methods, and to indicate possible outcomes. (p100-101)

This points, in the last sentence, to the value of the study of singularities which can give findings that, although not generalisable (and hence not suitable for the articulation of general theories), can enable individual teachers to relate to them, and hence to discover new possibilities for classroom action.

4. EXAMPLES OF STATEMENTS MADE AS OPEN GENERALISATIONS THAT SHOULD HAVE BEEN EXPRESSED AS CLOSED GENERALISATIONS

(a) **Bligh (1971)** *What's the Use of Lectures?*

In *What's the Use of Lectures?* Bligh (1971) summarised his analysis of 68 research reports on the effectiveness of lectures, compared to other methods of transmitting information, in this statement:

> The lecture is as effective as other methods for transmitting information.

Chapter Six ON SEARCH FOR GENERALISATIONS

This purports to be an open generalisation. In fact it is not a valid statement at all. In his analysis he found 16 reports in which lectures were more effective than other methods in transmitting information, 14 reports in which lectures were less effective and 38 reports in which the results showed no significant differences between lectures and other methods.

I suggest that he should have expressed his results as a closed generalisation, perhaps like this:

> In 68 studies carried out up to 1971 it was found in over a half that the lecture is no more and no less effective than other methods for transmitting information. However in just under a quarter of these studies the lecture was found to be more effective and in a similar number it was found to be less effective.

It has the disadvantage of being over five times longer, lacks punch and so is less memorable, but, unlike the cited statement, it is accurate!

(b)   Bennett (1975) *Teaching Styles and Pupil Progress*

In Teaching Styles and Pupil Progress, Bennett (1976) formulated conclusions in the form of open generalisations, viz:

> The results form a coherent pattern. The effect of teaching style is statistically and educationally significant in all attainment areas tested. In reading, pupils of formal and mixed teachers progress more than those of informal teachers, the difference being equivalent to some three to five months' difference in performance. In mathematics formal pupils are superior to both mixed and informal pupils ...

These conclusions had a tremendous impact, being used by some politicians and newspapers as a massive indictment of informal styles in schools. [Later Bennett modified his conclusions on re-analysis of the data]. Would the following statement, written as a closed generalisation have had the same impact?

> The results *from 37 teachers (selected from 468, 4th year junior school teachers in Lancashire and Cumbria in 1974 to make three groups characterised as 'formal', 'mixed' and 'informal')* form a coherent pattern. The effect of teaching style *was* statistically and educationally significant in all attainment areas tested. In reading, *the* pupils of *the* formal and *the* mixed teachers progress*ed on average* more than those of *the* informal teachers, the difference being equivalent *on average* to some three to five months' difference in performance. In mathematics *on average the* formal pupils *were* superior to both mixed and informal pupils ...

The insertion of 'on average' is important because, as the researcher makes clear, not all of the thirteen informal teachers had worse results than the other teachers.

> The results presented so far portray a fairly dismal picture of achievement in informal classrooms. Nevertheless there was one such classroom which was categorised by high gain in every achievement area; indeed in one area it was the highest gain class.

It follows that the statements about formal and informal styles are not useful in predicting for any particular teacher the outcomes of these styles. There are other factors operating in the classroom: these statements may be helpful if seen as thinking points, but are unhelpful, if not worse, if seen as having the predictive power of open generalisation.

There is an important point to be made here about averaging. The fundamental unit in education is the individual person, but when researchers look for generalisation the individual is obscured and replaced by means, standard deviations, and more complicated statistical devices which further obliterate the individual. The argument is that this is necessary in order to draw conclusions from the data, but inevitably this conceals the evidence of any individuals who are different from the majority. Perhaps researchers should publish scattergrams showing the results from every individual as well as the averages. This would draw attention to anomalies.

(c) Recent thesis titles

The two examples above of expressing findings as an open generalisation instead of a closed generalisation are taken from the 1970s, where it was common practice. Today this is unlikely to be found in substantial research reports but is still prevalent in student endeavours. As an external examiner of MEd, MPhil and PhD dissertations and theses I frequently have to draw attention to this methodological flaw in reasoning. Consider the following two titles from a recent issue of the ASLIB Index of Theses.

> *The normative ethos of British secondary comprehensive schools: the religious connection.* [The abstract states that this was a study in three schools]

> *Sleeping beauties awoken? A study of the impact of the 1986 and 1988 education legislation on the operation of school governing bodies.* [The abstract indicates that this was a study of one school]

These can be contrasted with the following titles which make clear that they are studies of singularities:

> *Pupil behaviour and teacher reactions: a study of four Oxford comprehensive schools.*

> *The effects of a multicultural arts programme on the racial perceptions of a class of white 10 year old children.*

5. THE VALUE OF GENERALISATIONS FOR POLICY-MAKERS

In Chapter One the point was made that there are major, and quite different, audiences for educational research - two being practitioners and policy-makers. So far in this chapter it has been suggested that there is little profit to be gained in searching for generalisations which might help the work of practitioners. The reverse is true for policy-makers: they need generalisations and, provided researchers have adequate resources, sometimes this need can be met. Two examples are put forward here from recent research. Both featured in the preparation of the report of the National Commission on Education which was published in 1993.

(a) Osborn A F and Milbank J E (1987) *The Effects of Early Education*

In Great Britain in the week 5-11 April 1970 about 16,200 children were born: this research was based on evidence from 12,051 of them. Thus a sample of about 1 in 50 of the generation born in 1970 was used. Although on this scale it might be expected that findings from the sample could be reliably attributed to the whole population this may not be the case since children born at different times of the year may get different amounts of schooling during their infant years, and seasonal weather may have a bearing on the experience of the first year of life which may influence later development. This cohort of children are regularly studied by a Bristol University group known as the Child Health and Education Study Research Team. This particular report is based on evidence collected when the children were 5 and 10.

The summary statement in the Introduction to this report says:
> The findings from the study showed that children who attended preschool institutions achieved higher test scores at 5 and 10 years than others who had no preschool experience. (p1)

How valid is this generalisation?

The 294 pages of the report are not easy reading for anyone trying to decide whether the evidence substantiates this conclusion. The two tables in Figure [8] are extracted from more complicated tables given in the report. They relate pre-school education to ability in reading and mathematics at age ten. More precisely they show for the four largest groups by which the children's pre-school experience was analysed (none, LEA nursery class attached to an infant school, LEA nursery school, and playgroup meeting in a hall) the average results gained by 10 year-olds on a reading test (shortened version of the Edinburgh reading test which tested vocabulary, syntax, sequencing and comprehension) and a mathematics test (72 multiple choice questions covering arithmetical processes, number concept,, geometry, algebra, trigonometry, and statistics).

In the first table the average results for each of the four categories of children are given, and it seems clear that those who have been to a nursery school or to a hall playgroup have done better than those with no pre-school experience. But is this cause and effect? And why do nursery classes (in a primary school) not show similar results to nursery schools? The important question that must be asked is whether it is the listed educational experience (or non-experience) that is responsible for the differences in reading and mathematical scores, or some other factors. The research team found, for example, that using 'a composite index of socio-economic inequality', which divided the sample into five equal-sized groups, 46% of the 'most disadvantaged' had received no form of pre-school education, compared to only 10% of the 'most advantaged' group. The research team said:

> We have adopted an essentially Popperian approach in our evaluation of preschool education services by attempting to refute the proposition that attendance at a preschool institution has a positive effect on children's cognitive development and educational attainment. To this end we have attempted to find as many intervening variables as possible which reduce the size and statistical strength of the associations between children's preschool experience and their test scores. (p210)

The outcome of this statistical analysis is the data in the second table of Figure [8].

Figure [8] Results from Osborn and Milbank

Table A. Average reading score and average mathematics score for four groups of children

child's experience	no. of children studied	average reading score	average mathematics score
no pre-school	3380	96.2	96.8
LEA nursery class	1027	97.0	96.9
LEA nursery school	596	100.5	100.5
hall playgroup	2954	103.4	103.1

Table B. Average reading score and average mathematics score for four groups of children adjusted for social index score, type of neighbourhood and number of children in the household

child's experience	no. of children studied	average reading score	average mathematics score
no pre-school	3380	98.2	98.3
LEA nursery class	1027	98.9	98.8
LEA nursery school	596	100.7	100.8
hall playgroup	2954	100.9	100.7

Chapter Six ON SEARCH FOR GENERALISATIONS

One difficulty in reading this report is to understand the phrase 'adjusted for social index score, type of neighbourhood and number of children in the household'. How can we be sure that these statistical adjustments are valid? For example, did the social index score adjustment completely eliminate the influence of socio-economic differences in the children's home backgrounds? Can we be sure that this is something that can be effectively measured, and if so, was it effectively measured by the research team on this large population? Another difficulty is in understanding the meaning of the scores. For example is 98.2 as an average score for one group very different from 100.9 for another? In terms of the ability of ten-year-olds to read what does it mean?

This report was not published until 1987, seven years after the testing at age ten and twelve years after the end of the pre-school period for the cohort of children. In recognising this the authors say:

> changes in practice in the preschool institutions attended by the children in our study in 1973-75 would have been introduced in order to increase the quality of the educational experience provided, and therefore the long-term benefits that we have observed are likely to be even greater for children currently enrolling in preschool institutions. (p241)

By the end of the report the claim of association between pre-school experience and higher test scores later, as quoted above from page 1, is turned into a claim of consequence. Thus on the final page, the authors say:

> preschool education will in most circumstances aid the child's development, increase his educational potential and in the long run his overall performance. (p242)

This claim that preschool education will have the consequence of increasing overall performance later is based on the failure to find any other explanation for the findings.

This brief account of the study by Osborn and Milbank shows some of the difficulties of making generalisations which will impress policy makers. The Report of the National Commission on Education (1993) gives as its first goal: high-quality nursery education must be available for all 3- and 4-year-olds (p397). The Commission based this recommendation on much wider evidence than that cited above, but nevertheless recognised the need for stronger evidence, in these words.

> Those who wish to expand and improve pre-school education are under pressure to justify any claims for increased resources by demonstrating that better services will result in measurable long-term benefits. ... A specially-designed and well-controlled longitudinal research project would be required in order to provide reliable evidence, and such a study has not yet been carried out in this country. (p114)

(b) Keys W and Fernandes C (1993) *What Do Students Think About School?*

This report was commissioned by the National Commission on Education in order to ascertain the views of young people themselves about their experiences in schools today. The research was carried out by the National Foundation for Educational Research during the summer term 1992. It involved questionnaires to Year 7 and Year 9 pupils and covered the following main topics:

> **background variables including:** gender, surrogate measures intended to provide an approximate indication of the cultural level of the home; perceived ability and behaviour in school; and post-16 educational intentions;
>
> **attitudes towards school and learning including:** views about the value of school and school work; liking for school; interest and boredom with school work; and opinions on the purposes of schooling;
>
> **perceptions of teachers and lessons including:** liking for teachers; teachers' support of students' learning; teachers' maintenance of discipline; individual discussions with teachers about school work and career plans; and liking for different types of lessons;
> students' self-reported behaviour in and out of school including: behaviour in school; punishments; truancy; participation in lunch hour or after school activities; length of time spent doing homework, reading for pleasure; and watching television or videos;
>
> **perceptions of parental interest and home support including:** parents' opinions about the value of education; parental interest in students' progress at school; parental encouragement of good behaviour in school; parental aspirations; discussion of career plans with their parents, family and friends. (Keys and Fernandes 1993 ppI-6 to I-7)

The questionnaires were completed by 1160 Year 7 students in 47 schools and 980 Year 9 students in 43 schools. The account of how these pupils were selected and then validated as effective samples is an object lesson in professional sampling. Two groups of 75 schools were identified by a stratified random sampling of all the secondary schools in England and Wales. The stratification was by size (numbers of pupils in the age group to be studied), type of school (comprehensive to 16, comprehensive to 18, other state secondary, independent), region (north, midlands, south), and type of LEA (metropolitan, non-metropolitan). It was expected that about two-thirds of these would agree to participate, and this was the case. In each school one tutor group was randomly selected and all of the pupils asked to complete the questionnaire. Background data from the pupil responses, and data from the schools, was assessed to show that the students sampled were likely to be representative of all their age

Chapter Six ON SEARCH FOR GENERALISATIONS

group in England and Wales and that the two samples (Year 7 and Year 9) showed no significant differences in relevant parameters.

The outcome of the research was important in refuting a common view of widespread disenchantment with schools. It was expressed by the National Commission report in this paragraph.

> The extent of poor achievement and negative attitudes is commonly misrepresented in public discussion. Sometimes the media give the impression that secondary schools are heavily populated with discontented pupils who find schooling irrelevant, and who show their disenchantment by disruptive behaviour, poor attendance and by leaving school as soon as the law permits. The Commission's own survey ... tells a different story. The majority of these pupils demonstrated high expectations of learning and strong support for the value of schools. ... Over 90% thought that school work was worth doing and more than 75% said that on the whole they liked being at school. (p151)

The National Commission balanced this picture by referring to the findings on disenchantment.

> There is also a clear indication that a significant minority of pupils are hostile to school by the end of the first year in secondary school. Eight per cent of 11-year-olds in the survey found all or most of their lessons boring and 12% said they did not like being at school. (p152)

The NFER report had some important evidence on teaching and learning practices. For example:

> The study identified quite strong associations between student's attitudes and a range of aspects of teaching behaviour. High expectations on the part of the teacher, regular feedback, praise for good work and effective classroom discipline were shown to be associated with students' positive attitudes towards school and education. This finding is not new. The previous research described in our review of the literature, found similar results and most educationalists are aware of the importance of these factors. However, the results of our research suggest that many teachers were not lavish with praise, that a minority of teachers were 'fairly easily satisfied' and that many pupils did not talk individually with their teachers about their work. (Keys and Fernandes 1993, pI-65)

This last point is perhaps the most remarkable outcome of the research. 42% of the pupils claimed that they never talked to a teacher about their work.

*   *   *   *   *

Let us return to the concept of generalisation and to the need of policy makers for them. The above research outcome can be expressed like this:

> In years 7 and 9 in the schools of England and Wales in 1992, four pupils in every ten considered that they never talked with their teachers about their school work.

This generalisation can be induced from the survey because of the way in which the samples of respondents were obtained, and validated. It is a closed generalisation because it has a boundary round it of space and time, but the space within that enclosure is very large and contains several thousand secondary schools. It refers specifically to 1992, but unless there is some significant change there is no reason to believe that it will not be true in 1993 and for the rest of the century at least!

Such a generalisation seems to me to be a clarion call to national policy makers for action. Perhaps first they need to be convinced that individual discourse between teacher and pupil is worthwhile and may be a significant factor in the pupil's academic progress. Next they need to triangulate this evidence to ensure that the absence of such discourse is near to the truth and is not a widespread misconception by students. Then they need to find some of the reasons for this gulf between pedagogic expectation and classroom practice. The next stage is to identify and implement strategies to remedy the situation, and finally the policy makers need to commission an evaluative study, using the same NFER questions and careful sampling, to ascertain whether there has been change in the direction they seek.

This generalisation is unlikely to be of practical use to individual teachers. To many of them it will not apply, and to those to whom it does apply it is unlikely to make any impact on their practice, for they will say 'Circumstances unfortunately prevent me from doing this thing which I know would be worthwhile, and I am comforted to realise that four out of ten of my fellow teachers are in the same position'.

The audience for this research is policy-makers, not practitioners. Perhaps its title should have been a little longer, ie *What did year 7 and year 9 students think about their schools in England and Wales in 1992?* This is less punchy, but more precise, and it draws attention to the need for further studies - such as of year 11 and year 13 pupils, and of repeats in future years to ascertain whether there has been progress.

*   *   *   *   *

In the next chapter we will examine the idea of study of singularity.

Chapter Seven

ON STUDY OF SINGULARITIES

Sections

1.	SINGULARITIES ENTAIL BOUNDARIES AROUND PARTICULAR EVENTS	110
2.	WHY 'SINGULARITY' AND NOT 'CASE STUDY'?	111
3.	EXAMPLES OF STUDIES OF SINGULARITIES, SEARCHES FOR GENERALISATION, AND REFLECTIVE STUDIES	113

He was a rather fierce teacher of physics in the traditional style of chalk-and-talk. 'Hands up who knows what electricity is,' he said. The class wriggled apprehensively. 'Come on, let's have an answer.' A small boy at the back put up his hand. 'Please sir. I did know, but I've forgotten.' 'Dear oh dear,' said the teacher. 'The only person in the whole world who has ever known what electricity is - and he's forgotten.'

Does this anecdote, this account of a singularity, have meaning beyond that classroom at that time? I think so.

1. SINGULARITIES ENTAIL BOUNDARIES AROUND PARTICULAR EVENTS

A study of a singularity is research into particular events.

Before pursuing this further, we should reflect on the concept of a singularity. Let us start with the idea of a social event, or incident, or happening, or occurrence (I take these to mean the same). The *event* involves one or more people at a particular place and a particular time having a particular experience. Note that the adjective being used is 'particular' and not 'unique'. 'Particular' means having its own characteristics and these characteristics can be related to other people, places, times and experiences. Thus if I tell you that three ten-year-old boys were playing tag on a railway station and one fell onto the track, you have points of reference which enable you to relate your own understanding to this *particular* event. But if I tell you that three ten-year-old boys were xenollated by a sphercon you are (presumably) unable to understand what happened in this *unique* event. In other words we are concerned with particular events and not unique ones.

If a particular event is described to other people (which means that someone judges it worth drawing to their attention), either in speech or writing, it becomes an *anecdote*. The anecdote is a means of telling other people, who had not been present, what happened. (Often, of course, an anecdote is humorous, but the term has a much wider meaning, which is being used here, to refer to the story of particular events).

When we decide that something is sufficiently significant to warrant being researched, it is usually not just one particular event but a set of related particular events that are the focus of interest. This means a set of events around which a boundary can be drawn. Strictly speaking, of course, it is the anecdotes describing the events with which we are concerned. The boundary can be defined in space and time, for example as a particular classroom, or school, or local education authority, or as sets of these, in a particular period; or it may be defined as a particular person, or group of people, at a particular time and in a particular space.

Thus at the point when it becomes the subject of study, a singularity is a set of anecdotes about particular events occurring within a stated boundary, which are subjected to systematic and critical search for some truth. This truth, while pertaining to the inside of the boundary, may stimulate thinking about similar situations elsewhere.

The search for truth will seek answers to some research question, maybe a research hypothesis that is being tested, or a research problem that is being probed, or a research issue that is being explored.

While the empirical conclusion of the study of the singularity should remain within the boundary, it is quite proper and appropriate for the researcher to include in the research report (perhaps under the heading of 'reflections', or 'discussion' or 'general conclusion') views on how the findings may relate to situations outside the boundary. The empirical conclusion should be as truthful a statement about events within the boundary as the researcher can devise. The extrapolation of this empirical conclusion beyond the boundary is a matter of speculation. The point about the relatability of findings from one situation to another is that there is no surety that they can be applied, but the merit of the comparison is that it may stimulate worthwhile thinking.

To some people the distinction between a study of a singularity and a search for generalisation is pedantic and unnecessary. In terms of the research ethic of the pursuit of truth, I disagree. The conclusions of research should only be generalised, meaning that they are firmly extrapolated beyond the population under study, if it is clearly established that the general population has the same characteristics as the population which has been researched. To assume that the findings from one study of a small group of primary school teachers, or fifteen-year-old children, or left-handed astrologers with blonde hair, can be extrapolated to others who fit the same description is nonsense! It is nonsense because there are so many other contextual variables which may determine what happens - variables of personal history, of understanding and of intention of all of the actors involved, as well as variables of setting.

2. WHY 'SINGULARITY' AND NOT 'CASE STUDY'?

My reason for preferring the description 'study of a singularity' rather than 'case study' is because, as Adelman, Jenkins and Kemmis (1980, p49) put it some time ago, 'the term *case study* remains a slippery one.' They saw it as an umbrella term for a family of research methods having in common the decision to focus on enquiry around an instance. (p48)

Cohen and Manion (1980) in their authoritative text *Research Methods in Education*, say this of case study (and repeat it in the 3rd edition of 1989).

> Unlike the experimenter who manipulates variables to determine their causal significance or the surveyor who asks standardised questions of large representative samples of individuals, the case study researcher typically observes the characteristics of an individual unit - a child, a clique, a class, a school, or a community. The purpose of such observation is to probe deeply and to analyse intensively the multifarious phenomena that constitute the life cycle of the unit with a view to establishing generalisations about the wider population to which that unit belongs. (p99)

Those who agree with my argument earlier in this chapter about the problems of generalisation will share my concern about the emphasis that Cohen and Manion put on case study leading to generalisation.

Adelman, Jenkins and Kemmis (p49) identified two types of case study. In the first type there is a general issue being enquired into and a case study is made as an example of all the cases where this general issue arises. (This is the type cited by Cohen and Manion) In their second type the starting point is what they call 'the bounded system', ie the case, and a local issue is enquired into for the purpose of gaining greater understanding of the local issue.

In 1976 I organised a research project in which 893 teachers in 114 Nottinghamshire primary schools were asked a schedule of questions which aimed to find out about their major practices used in their classrooms and schools (Bassey 1978). It might stretch interpretation too far to see this as a 'case study', but I certainly saw it as a 'study of a singularity' because there was a clear boundary in space and time for the project and its purpose was to inform other primary teachers of the different ways in which this group of teachers operated, not to draw general statements about primary education in England. (Indeed I have felt irritated when this study has been quoted by other researchers as though it were representative of the country as a whole!)

I consider that the term 'study of a singularity' embraces virtually every kind of empirical study other than where the subjects of study have been carefully selected as a representative sample of some population about which it is intended to make general statements. Thus most experiments, surveys, evaluations, case studies, and action researches come under this heading.

The term originates in an educational context, as far as a I am aware, in the title of the book, edited by Simons (1980) called *Towards a Science of the Singular*. She attributes the term to the inspiration of David Hamilton.

3. EXAMPLES OF STUDIES OF SINGULARITIES, SEARCHES FOR GENERALISATION, AND REFLECTIVE STUDIES

In Chapter Three a number of papers were cited, and their abstracts reproduced, to develop the idea of there being distinctions between educational research and research in various social science disciplines in educational settings. Here I have analysed these papers, in a different categorisation, into studies of singularities, searches for generalisation, and reflective studies. In addition the monographs of Osborn and Milbank (1987) and Keys and Fernandes (1993), which feature in Chapter Six are included.

My categorisation is based on a rigorous consideration of any empirical data collected by the researchers. If the researchers are using data collected by others, or analysing documents, I have categorised their research as in the *reflective* realm of research, as described in Chapter One. If the researchers have collected data themselves (ie the study comes within the *empirical* realm of research) and it entailed a rigorous sampling which was representative of a larger population, then I have categorised their research as *search for generalisation*. In cases where data has been collected that is not a rigorous sampling of a larger population, irrespective of whether the authors have attempted to generalise their findings, I have categorised the research as *study of a singularity*. I have used the technical term *relate* to express any link that authors have made with populations beyond the cases studied.

The numbers in square brackets give page numbers in this book to the earlier discussion of these papers.

Studies of singularities - some examples

> **Some sink, some float: National Curriculum assessment and accountability** Abbott D, Broadfoot P, Croll P, Osborn M, and Pollard A (1994) *British Educational Research Journal* 20(2) 155-174 [p41]

Comment. The *boundary* to the empirical data collected surrounded three year 2 classrooms in different local education authorities (LEAs) in 1991 where the same standard assessment task

(SAT) was observed in use. The paper *relates* the findings to the situation throughout England and suggests that the national assessment system is flawed.

Teaching the Holocaust: the relevance of children's perceptions of Jewish culture and identity Short G (1994) *British Educational Research Journal* 20(4) 393-405 [p41]

Comment. The *boundary* to the empirical data collected was around 'seventy-two children aged between 12 and 14'. It is not clear when they were interviewed. The paper *relates* the findings to teaching about the Holocaust in the history curriculum of 11-14-year olds in all maintained schools in England and Wales.

Teacher perceptions of their needs as mentors in the context of developing school-based initial teacher education. Williams A (1993) *British Educational Research Journal* 19 (4) 407-420.

Comment. The *boundary* to the empirical data collected surrounded 101 secondary school teachers (location and time not stated) that were supervising PGCE students and who replied to a questionnaire (66% response rate). The paper *relates* the findings to 'future initial teacher education programmes'.

Group child interviews as a research tool. Lewis A (1992) *British Educational Research Journal* 18 (4) 413-421 [p42]

Comment. The *boundary* to the empirical data collected was around a group of nine 10-year-old children. The paper *relates* the findings to the general situation of group interviews with children.

Teachers' careers and comprehensive school closure: policy and professionalism in practice. Riseborough G F (1994) *British Educational Research Journal* 20(1), 85-104 [p43]

Comment. The *boundary* to the empirical data collected was around 'two secondary school teachers in an urban working-class school'. The paper *relates* the findings to aspects of career structures, institutional closure, crises of motivation, social class and the New Right.

Governors, Schools and the Miasma of the Market Deem R, Brehony K, and Heath S (1994) *British Educational Research Journal* 20(5) 535-549 [p45]

Chapter Seven ON STUDY OF SINGULARITIES

Comment. The *boundary* to the empirical data collected surrounded the governing bodies of three secondary schools in two local education authorities during 1989-93. The paper *relates* the findings to the possible consequences of market-oriented competition between schools in general.

Arguing for yourself: identity as an organising principle in teachers' jobs and lives. Maclure M (1993) *British Educational Research Journal* 19 (4) 311-322 [p46]

Comment. The *boundary* to the empirical data collected enclosed a group of 69 primary and secondary school teachers in the period 1987-90. The paper *relates* the findings to general ideas about identity.

Computer anxiety in primary schoolchildren and university students Todman J and Lawrenson H (1992) *British Educational Research Journal* 18(1) 63-72 [p46]

Comment. The *boundary* to the empirical data collected was around a group of 20 first-year psychology students and a group of 29 nine-year-old children of comparable intelligence in about 1990. The paper *relates* the findings to the general population by suggesting that there is an absence of a strong link between computer anxiety (CA) and mathematics anxiety (MA).

The management of children in the dining room at lunch-time. Busby S (1991) (In Lomax, P (ed) *Managing better schools and colleges: an action research way,* BERA Dialogues, Multilingual Matters, Clevedon, England) [p48]

Comment. The *boundary* to the empirical data collected enclosed one 'large multi-ethnic primary school in London' in the school year 1989-90 where the author taught. The findings may *relate* to situations in which other teachers find themselves.

The implementation and evaluation of a drama course for all secondary pupils in a comprehensive school Rushworth L (1993) in Turner, D (ed) *Research in action,* Pavic Publications, Sheffield, England [p50]

Comment. The *boundary* to the empirical data collected was around the drama department of a secondary school where the author taught in 1988-9. The findings may *relate* to situations in which other teachers find themselves.

> **Language counts in the teaching of mathematics** Wright, S (1990) in Webb, R (ed) *Practitioner research in the primary school*, Falmer Press, Basingstoke, England [p50]

Comment. The *boundary* to the empirical data collected enclosed six 'middle infants' in a primary school where the researcher taught part-time. The findings may *relate* to situations in which other teachers find themselves.

Searches for generalisations - some examples

> **The curriculum for English 15-year-old pupils in 1984. Was there a common core of subjects?** Bell J F (1990) *British Educational Research Journal* 16 (1) 41-52 [p47]

Comment. The *boundary* to the empirical data was around all 15-year-old pupils in England in 1984. This population was rigorously *sampled*. 'The sample of approximately 7500 pupils and 266 schools was nationally representative, including all types of secondary, state-maintained and independent schools. The data were gathered in November 1984.' 'The main finding of this paper is that, on the basis of subject uptake, no pupil in the sample was studying a combination that satisfied all the requirements of the national curriculum proposal.' The author doesn't make a more general statement, but on the evidence of the paper, the *generalisation* 'No' would be a legitimate and rigorous answer to the question posed in the title.

> *The Effects of Early Education* Osborn A F and Milbank J E (1987) [pp105-108]

Comment. The *boundary* to the empirical data was around the 16,200 children born in Great Britain in the week 5-11 April 1970, of whom data was collected in 1975 and 1980 on about 12,051. As discussed in Chapter Six on page 1 of the monograph the following is claimed.

> The findings from the study showed that children who attended preschool institutions achieved higher test scores at 5 and 10 years than others who had no preschool experience.

This is a *closed generalisation* because it lies within the sample. However at the end of the monograph (p242) the authors express an *open generalisation* that:

> preschool education will in most circumstances aid the child's development, increase his educational potential and in the long run his overall performance.

The rigour of stepping beyond the sample to make this open generalisation (not limited in time or location) is questionable.

Chapter Seven   ON STUDY OF SINGULARITIES

What Do Students Think About School? Keys W and Fernades C (1993) [p108]

Comment. The *boundary* to the empirical data surrounded all year 7 and year 9 pupils in school in England and Wales during the summer term of 1992. This population was rigorously sampled. The findings can be expressed as a *closed generalisation* thus:

> In years 7 and 9 in the schools of England and Wales in 1992, four pupils in every ten considered that they never talked with their teachers about their school work.

Reflective studies - some examples

Value-added attacks: technical issues in reporting national curriculum assessments. Wiliam D (1992) *British Educational Research Journal* 18 (4) 329-341 [p42]

Underachievement: a case of conceptual confusion. Plewis I (1991) *British Educational Research Journal* 17 (4) 377-385 [p43]

What happens when a school subject undergoes a sudden change of status? Paechter C (1993) *Curriculum Studies* 1(3), 349-363 [p44]

Alternative perspectives of the nature of mathematics and their influence on the teaching of mathematics. Lerman S (1990) *British Educational Research Journal* 16 (1) 53-61 [p47]

Comment. Reading the abstracts makes clear that these papers do not start from empirical data collected by the authors, but are predominantly based on critical review and logical argument.

*   *   *   *   *   *

I hope that this account of 18 studies makes clear why I assert that a study of a singularity is research into particular events whose findings may be related to other situations, but should not be generalised. It also illustrates the merit of the suggestion developed in Chapter Five, that there be a specific heading in a report of empirical research entitled 'Empirical Conclusion' with a subsequent section developing any possibility of this being related, or extrapolated to other educational situations. This is an important aspect of any consideration of quality in research, which is the subject of the next chapter.

Chapter Eight

ON QUALITY IN RESEARCH IN EDUCATION

Sections

1. WHAT ARE THE CHARACTERISTICS OF QUALITY IN RESEARCH IN EDUCATION?   119

2. EXPLORING QUALITY IN TERMS OF THE EXPECTATIONS OF A DOCTORAL THESIS IN EMPIRICAL RESEARCH IN EDUCATION   122

3. EXPLORING QUALITY IN TERMS OF THE EXPECTATIONS OF AN ACADEMIC PAPER   124

Chapter Eight ON QUALITY IN RESEARCH IN EDUCATION

It sounds an unlikely tale, but it is said that the young Albert Einstein was a late developer in talking and caused his parents much worry because of his lack of speech. Suddenly, during a meal he said, 'Die Suppe ist sehr heiss'. Flabbergasted, but delighted at this utterance of a complete sentence, his mother asked, 'Albert, why have you never spoken before?' He answered, 'There has been nothing to say before.'

Quality is a vital issue!

1. WHAT ARE THE CHARACTERISTICS OF QUALITY IN RESEARCH IN EDUCATION?

A shepherd and a goatherd are unlikely to agree on the quality of their animals for one will be looking for wool and the other for milk. It is the same with discussions on the quality of research in education. Educational researchers, sociological researchers, psychological researchers, and others working in educational settings are looking for different things. Hence it is necessary to establish some common ground before examining issues of quality.

Suppose that the various ways of conducting research in education that are described as topography and deep structure in Chapter One and developed further in Chapters Six and Seven are all seen as potentially open to investigations of high quality. Suppose that the ethics of Chapter One are accepted, so that violation would be deemed as lack of quality. Suppose that the definitions of educational research, and of sociological, psychological, historical, and philosophical research in education in Chapter Three are agreed and that it is accepted that each of these has the potential for work of high quality. Suppose that the methodological ideas of Chapters Four and Five are acceptable. What then?

Perhaps it is obvious that, in the language of research, *quality* is a qualitative construct and not a quantitative one. It can be described, but not measured. It can be discussed, but not defined with precision. I propose to discuss quality first in terms of *adventurousness in the choice of topic*. Secondly, to discuss quality in terms of intellectual rigour in conducting enquiry and in reporting findings, or to put it another way, *elegance of the process*. Thirdly, to discuss quality in terms of the significance and worthwhileness of the findings, or *worthwhileness of the product*.

Quality in adventurousness in the choice of topic

Quality in this respect lies in the extent to which significant insights can be expected from the research. It implies that the outcome should be worthwhile; that somehow it will change the world in some theoretical, or practical, or policy-making way. It also implies that the project is viable, that it can be executed with the resources available, for successful adventurers are not foolhardy.

This is discussed at greater length in Chapter Nine.

Quality in elegance of the process of research

Quality requires each decision made in conducting research to be rigorously based on an acceptable rationale, and it requires each assertion made in reporting research to be rigorously based on acceptable evidence.

It follows that quality can be expected:

(a) in the framing of the research questions which define the purpose of the enquiry, and in the reformulation of these as circumstances change;

(b) in the appropriateness of the rationale or theory which underpins the enquiry;

(c) in the choice of setting and definition of the boundary if the enquiry is a study of a singularity;

(d) in the representativeness of the sample if the enquiry is a search for generalisation;

(e) in the way in which data is systematically recorded, stored, and is potentially available for audit;

(f) in the extent to which the data are perceived as trustworthy, and are as accurate as necessary;

(g) in the extent to which the interpretations, explanations and conclusions arise logically and rationally from analysis of the data;

(h) in terms of the enquiry being perceived as ethical;

(i) in the extent to which the researchers have been self-critical of their methods and through this have improved the value of their findings;

(j) in the extent to which the researchers have developed and justified new methods of enquiry;

(k) in the clarity and lucidity with which the account of the research and its claim to knowledge are expressed,

(l) in a study of a singularity in the way in which the empirical conclusion is rigorously framed and then related to similar situations;

(m) in a search for generalisation in the way in which the empirical conclusion is rigorously framed in relation to both the sample and the general population; and

(n) in the extent to which as wide an audience as may benefit from the new knowledge will have the opportunity of access to the publication.

Judgements of quality such as these are clearly pertinent to all forms of research in educational settings (and, of course, elsewhere).

Quality in worthwhileness of the product of research

Quality in the worthwhileness of the product of research is about the value of the claim to knowledge that results from research. It is here that the identification of different kinds of research in educational settings, as teased out in Chapter Three, becomes important. These different kinds of research have different ends, and so have different criteria for assessing quality. Thus they need to be examined separately. Nevertheless, in these kinds of research, there is likely to be a common view of the distinction between the pedestrian and the significant.

Pedestrian research will add a small increment to the existing accumulation of knowledge; significant research, for example, may challenge existing theory, offer novel insights of potential power, put forward a new method of enquiry, or integrate previously fragmented understandings. If pedestrian research is compared to the writing of footnotes in a book, significant research is the writing of new chapters or the rewriting of old ones.

Quality in *educational research* is concerned with the extent to which the outcomes of research have a significant and worthwhile effect on the judgements and decisions of practitioners or policy-makers towards improving educational action. Excellence entails the potential for heralding substantial change in educational practice, or educational policy making.

Quality in *sociological research in education* is concerned with the extent to which the outcomes of research make a significant and worthwhile contribution to understanding of social phenomena. Excellence entails the potential for substantial development in theory.

Quality in *psychological research in education* is concerned with the extent to which the outcomes of research make a significant and worthwhile contribution to understanding of psychological phenomena. Excellence entails the potential for substantial development in theory.

Similar statements apply for historical research in education, philosophical research in education, etc., and in each case excellence entails the potential for substantial development in theory.

2. EXPLORING QUALITY IN TERMS OF THE EXPECTATIONS OF A DOCTORAL THESIS IN EMPIRICAL RESEARCH IN EDUCATION

A doctoral thesis is the culmination of at least three years of full-time study (or a longer period of part-time study) in which a research student is expected to demonstrate that s/he has become thoroughly trained in research methodology relevant to a substantial claim to knowledge made and substantiated in the thesis. The evidence that the claim to knowledge is based on systematic, critical and self-critical enquiry, is expected to be paraded in much more detail than would be put in an article for an academic journal.

By examining the expectations of a doctoral thesis we can identify a number of aspects of quality which elaborate on the lists given above.

A first essential is finding a suitable topic which can lead to the identification of research questions which are novel, significant, substantial, and potentially answerable within the limitations of time and resource available to the student.

Quality is expected

(a) in the choice of topic and the framing of research questions.

A second essential is a thorough examination and exposition of the context of the topic. This usually means the preparation of a comprehensive review of relevant literature. There are a number of pointers to quality which arise here.

Quality is expected

(b) in the effectiveness of the trawl of the literature in searching for relevant items and the methodological account of this;
(c) in the thoroughness of going back to original sources wherever possible rather than citing second-hand descriptions;
(d) in the accuracy of reporting the findings of other researchers;
(e) in the power and logic of the analysis of these items in relation to the claim to knowledge which is made in the thesis; and
(f) in the technical competence in citation.

Quality in citation deserves elaboration. It entails the possibility of easily finding any reference in the original literature. (Thus page numbers of the original literature are important where quotations are used, or specific ideas cited). It entails the possibility of easily finding in the thesis any citation made in the list of references. (Thus page numbers of the thesis should be cross-referenced in the list of references). It entails a consistency of style in terms of use of punctuation and parenthesis (for example in a systematic use of the Harvard system).

A third essential is that the methods of enquiry are carefully described.

> Quality is expected
> (g) in the rationale given for the methods chosen for the research and for any methods which were rejected;
> (h) in the account of the extent to which the chosen methods draw on the work of earlier research workers;
> (i) in the description of the methods; and
> (j) in the critique of the methods used.

(The first three of these usually appear early in a thesis; (j) is often put towards the end).

Often in research there are sensitive issues concerning the ethic of respect for persons in relation, for example, to the ownership of data and the intended dissemination of findings. In such cases:

> Quality is expected
> (k) in the design, use, and possible critique, of ethical guidelines for the collection and analysis of data, and the reporting of findings.

A fourth essential is that at least a representative selection of the raw data collected is given. For example there may be tables of responses from questionnaires, or transcripts of interview records, or sample of fieldnotes.

> Quality is expected
> (l) in the extent to which the credibility of the research process is assured through review of selections of raw data.

This indication of quality is helped if there is a listing (probably in an appendix) of the data collected and a reference to the archive in which this data is systematically and safely stored.

A fifth essential is an account of the analytical process by which the raw data were turned into findings and conclusions.

Quality is expected

> (m) in the appropriateness, elegance, effectiveness, perhaps novelty, of the analytical process and the thorough substantiation of any conclusions drawn;
>
> (n) in the extent to which meaningful connections are made to the existing literature; and
>
> (o) in the exactness of the claim to knowledge being either (i) a claim within the boundaries of space and time of the singularity studied, or (ii) a general claim in which case the representativeness of the sample studied is demonstrated.

A sixth essential is reflective critique of the research, possibly with pointers to further enquiry.

> Quality is expected
>
> (p) in the extent to which methodological errors and lost opportunities of hindsight are noted.

Finally comes the essential requirement that the thesis be presented as a perfect piece of writing and constructed within the guidelines laid down by the examining institution.

> Quality is expected
>
> (q) in the lucidity of expression, the awareness of potential audience, correctness of English, and aesthetic appearance of the text.

3. EXPLORING QUALITY IN TERMS OF THE EXPECTATIONS OF AN ACADEMIC PAPER

Many of the expectations of an academic paper are the same as for a doctoral thesis - but the space which editors will give authors is much less! In consequence the systematic, critical and self-critical description of the collection and analysis of data is necessarily shorter and in particular the extensive and personal justification of research decisions, which is a major feature of many research theses, is omitted. The following four quality arenas are pertinent to editors and referees.

> Quality may be judged to be sufficient to merit publication of the paper:
>
> (a) if the claim to new knowledge is clearly expressed;

(b) if the claim to new knowledge is set effectively in the context of existing knowledge;

(c) if the claim to new knowledge is clearly substantiated; and

(d) if the claim to new knowledge is judged to be sufficiently worthwhile to merit dissemination.

* * * * *

A number of these issues are related to the discussion of the next chapter, which asks 'What is significant, what is trivial?'

****

Chapter Nine

ON TRIVIAL PURSUITS AND SIGNIFICANT INSIGHTS

****

Sections

1.	INDIVIDUALISM AND TRIVIAL PURSUITS IN RESEARCH	127
2.	SIGNIFICANT INSIGHTS IN RESEARCH IN EDUCATION	133

Chapter Nine ON TRIVIAL PURSUITS AND SIGNIFICANT INSIGHTS

Pedro was looking out of the classroom window. His friends warned him, 'If she catches you looking out of the window she'll give you a piece of paper and tell you to write about it.' But they were wrong. The teacher said to him, 'Pedro. You have been looking out of the window most of this morning. What are you doing?' 'Miss. I'm thinking about how to save the world.' 'Oh', she replied, 'When you've done that how will you spend the afternoon?'

1. INDIVIDUALISM AND TRIVIAL PURSUITS IN RESEARCH

In the higher education system of the United Kingdom some of the funding of research in education comes from the Economic and Social Research Council (whose money originates from government) on the basis of proposals made by researchers (either in response to initiatives of the Council indicating areas that it seeks research in, or in response to initiatives of the researchers on areas of their own choice). Some funding comes from a number of large charities (for example Leverhulme, Nuffield) in response to researchers' initiatives, and some from government departments, government agencies, and local government, in response to the sponsors' interests. Decisions on the provision of these kinds of funding are based on the quality of proposals made by researchers and these judgements are usually made by peers. In total in 1994/5 I estimate this to be between £4 and £6 million in terms of research in education.

However the bulk of the funding of research in higher education comes into the institutions by a different route and different judgemental process. The Higher Education Funding Councils in 1994/5 put £27 million into research in education in the universities and colleges of the UK. The judgement as to how much funding should go to an individual institution is based on the number of active researchers and the assessment of their research effort in the recent past. Regular 'research assessment exercises' are held (1992 was the last, the next will be in 1996) and the quality of a department's research output is measured on a numerical scale, by a group of peers who act as consultants to the Funding Councils.

In the 1992 Research Assessment Exercise, 86 universities and colleges submitted returns in the area of Education. I was a member of the Education panel; we had an overview of research carried out by 1500 'active researchers', which gave a fascinating insight into much of the research in education being carried out in higher education institutions in this country.

What impact is this research making on the world of education? I asked this question after the formal exercise for the HEFCs was completed. I carried out a personal evaluation of this national output of research endeavours through a sample study of one fifth of the returns, and concluded that although there are some significant insights, overall the individualism and isolation of many of these researchers is unhelpful. There is too often a prevailing dilettante tradition of individual enquiry which looks like a game of trivial pursuits.

There is certainly some outstanding work giving significant insights, for example in constructivist learning, pupil assessment, school effectiveness, science education, and equal opportunities, but beyond this I am less certain that much of the research reported in the literature appreciably extends theory, or illuminates policy, or improves practice, in significant ways. I have a strong impression of individualism, of researchers working in isolation from each other, dabbling in a rather amateurish way at issues which are too big to be tackled by lone researchers.

It must be made clear that these strictures are mine alone. They are not the expressed opinion of either the Panel, the Higher Education Funding Councils, or the British Educational Research Association. Some individuals agree with me; others believe I have got it quite wrong.

Let me try to justify this polemical assertion. The procedure to be described was not part of the Research Assessment Exercise and was carried out by me after the results of the exercise had been announced. The data submitted by institutions was not to be revealed to other institutions and so the present data is anonymised.

I took a 20% sample of the 86 institutions. This was roughly representative of the whole list in terms of: rating in the HEFCs exercise, old universities vis-a-vis other institutions, the four countries of the United Kingdom, and number of academic staff in the institution doing research in education. In the submissions of these 12 institutions I highlighted all of the publications which were either authored books or articles in academic journals reporting on research. (The submissions contained, for each member of staff who was listed, two publications of the last four years - categorised by the institution as authored text, academic article, contribution to edited text, short publication, professional article, popular article, review, etc). My highlighted publications represented about 30% of the publications listed in my sample. I analysed them in terms of fields of enquiry and numbers of staff publishing academic papers in each of these fields.

The outcome of this analysis demonstrates the fragmentation of research effort. Crudely it suggests that of these researchers in education, a quarter are solitary workers, a half have three or fewer immediate colleagues working in the same field of research, and a quarter are working in research communities where they have four or more colleagues working in the same field of research. Of course, 'working in the same field' does not necessarily mean that researchers work co-operatively, or even talk to each other!

Figure [9] Fields of study of research in education identified in the publications of 17 UK institutions of higher education in 1988-1992

The table is in rank order with the fields with the highest numbers of publications at the top of the table.

School management
Science education
Teacher education
Information technology education
Language education
Overseas education
Mathematics education
Special education
Professional development
Classroom management
Educational policy
Assessment
Equal opportunities
Social education
Aesthetic education
Concept development
Health education
Technological education
Adult education
English education
Higher education
National curriculum
Research methodology
Child development
History of education
Moral education
Music education
Counselling
Environmental education
Religious education
Teacher stress
Business education
Community education
Creativity
Drama education
Further education
Nurse education
Nursery education
Parents
Physical education
Post-secondary education

The allocation into 'fields of enquiry' was inevitably problematic. Because of uncertainties in some cases as to which field a paper should be allocated, I am not indicating how many papers featured in each field. But I think the list of fields that I found (in my inevitably subjective identification of them) is of interest, because it gives an indication of what research in education was going on in universities in the UK in the period 1988-92. Admittedly this analysis is crude in terms of the selection of items and the allocation to fields of enquiry. It refers to permanent staff and not to contract researchers; it focuses only on academic publication; and it extrapolates from a fifth to the whole. But I submit that it highlights the dilettante tradition of much academic research, which sees the *involvement* in research as important, not the *outcome* of the research. The dilettante tradition stresses the act of searching for new knowledge, rather than the contribution which the new knowledge may make to theory, or to policy, or to practice. It values the singing, not the song.

A second analysis focuses on the number of authors per academic paper. Of the 362 academic papers in the analysis, 61% had a single author, 24% had two authors and 15% had three or more. Of the 142 papers with more than one author, 70% had an 'outsider' in the list of authors (meaning someone who was not a member of the academic staff of the institution).

It would help the argument if I were able to give at this point an example of the publication records under discussion, but this would breach the confidentiality of the Research Assessment Exercise. Instead I have invented a fictional record, as set out in Figure [10].

Figure [10] A fictional example of the academic publication record of a university department of education in the UK in the early 1990s

Adams	Group behaviour of 14 year-olds in problem solving classes in mathematics *Journal article*
Adams and Brown	Parental interest in the mathematics learned by their 7-11year-old children *Journal article*
Caxton and Clarke	Information technology and the teaching of English *Authored book*
Dickson	Drama workshops in special education *Authored book*
Edwards	Furniture design: a neglected dimension of classroom management *Journal article*
Fox	Bullying in the playground *Journal article*
Fox and McRae	Views on racism of student teachers in one college *Journal article*
Green	Creative and aesthetic education *Authored book*
Higgins and Jones	What 20 primary school teachers know about the solar system *Journal article*
King	Formative assessment in primary schools *Authored book*
King	'Value added' as an evaluative assessment tool *Journal article*
Lawson, McRae and Nixon	Variations of the lecture for undergraduate physics students *Journal article*
etc	etc

Chapter Nine ON TRIVIAL PURSUITS AND SIGNIFICANT INSIGHTS

In describing a research record like that in the table as 'trivial pursuits' I am not commenting on the competence of the research, for indeed there is no way that this can be judged from the titles of the publications. It is the likely impact of each piece of work that I see as 'trivial'. For example, it is very unlikely that 'Fox', working on his own, has discovered some fundamental truth about playground bullying that can with confidence be drawn to the attention of all schools and thereby enable them to reduce the incidence of bullying in their playgrounds. Or that the findings of 'Adams' can improve pedagogic practice in mathematics classrooms. Their solitary efforts are almost inevitably on too small a scale to result in significant insights.

Of course the traditional expectation is that the record in the literature of their solitary efforts will accumulate with other reports into similar situations, and somebody, somewhere, sometime will collate all of these into significant insights. But does this work effectively? I doubt it.

As an alternative, suppose that all fourteen of these people had worked for two years on the problems of playground bullying, under the leadership of 'Fox'. Suppose that they had observed many diverse incidents and conversed with children and teachers about them; suppose that they had discussed the bullying-reduction strategies of different schools and monitored the effectiveness of them; suppose that they had invited schools to try out strategies found successful elsewhere and, working in partnership with teachers engaging in action research, had evaluated these; suppose that they had systematically reviewed the literature and engaged in regular dialogue with others working in the same field; suppose that the outcome of the research efforts of these fourteen people working as a team for two years was one handbook for schools, a paper in a professional journal, and a series of academic papers in learned journals. Suppose that the research plan of the department allocated two years for this study and expected it to be followed by a similar period when everyone would work under say 'Adams' leadership on group behaviour of adolescents engaged in problem solving in mathematics classes.

Is this impossible? Are academics incapable of working co-operatively? Is the dilettante tradition so firmly entrenched that there is no alternative to trivial pursuits? In particular does the evaluation of research in an assessment exercise like the ones being conducted in the UK reinforce the dilettante tradition by focusing on publication of research rather than on its impact. I shall return to this shortly.

Perhaps you are saying: 'What is wrong with the dilettante tradition? Provided that the enquiry is conducted with academic rigour and the results are published in respected journals, does it matter that many people work alone?' Perhaps you are also saying: 'Teaching is the prime business of the universities and involvement in research is mainly something that sharpens the mind of the lecturer so that he or she teaches more effectively because of the experience of working at the frontier of knowledge.' You may even add: 'Fragmentation is valuable for it means that one department has experts in many fields related to teaching.'

If you are saying these things, I beg to differ. My reason is that society needs the focused intelligence of able people striving to tackle its educational problems. It is a moral argument as already explored in Chapter Two.

I believe this means that most researchers in education need to work in teams and networks. By 'team' I mean a substantial group of researchers within a department working co-operatively and effectively, so that they formulate clear research questions, attract adequate resources, know what progress is being made elsewhere, and devise and carry out effective strategies with which to pursue the questions. And having got somewhere, they make the results available to other researchers, and when appropriate to practitioners and policy-makers, with clarity and impact. By 'network' I mean an association of researchers from a number of institutions who regularly interact (probably using electronic mail) in carrying out research tasks on a particular issue.

The difficulty in this approach lies in the mores of the dilettante tradition. For example: the more publications produced the better; the more words written the better; the more times a paper is cited by others the better; single authorship is preferable to multiple scholarship; and academic journals read by researchers are more valued than professional journals read by teachers. These mores are in direct conflict with the views that I have expressed above. If the pun on 'more' and 'mores' jars, so I suggest should the dilettante tradition!

How can this tradition be changed? The answer could lie with the ways in which funding bodies evaluate research departments and allocate funds.

Suppose that a funding body, instead of judging a department by its list of publications, tried to use the three concepts discussed in the previous chapter and looked for ways of judging the quality of adventurousness in the chosen research topics, the quality of elegance in the conduct of research, and the quality of worthwhileness in the product. Adventurousness in the choice of research might be judged in terms of the extent to which the research programme of the department sets out in viable ways to change the world for the better in theoretical, or practical, or policy-making ways. Elegance in the conduct of research could be judged by careful reading of a sample of research reports emanating from the department, and assessing the extent to which these are based rigorously on an acceptable rationale, with each assertion

Chapter Nine ON TRIVIAL PURSUITS AND SIGNIFICANT INSIGHTS

arising firmly from acceptable evidence. Worthwhileness in the products of research could also be judged by sampling, but this time placing research reports somewhere on the continuum of significance from pedestrian to excellent. As suggested in Chapter Eight, pedestrian research will add a small increment to the existing accumulation of knowledge; excellent research, on the other hand, may challenge existing theory, or offer novel insights of potential power, or integrate previously fragmented understandings, for example.

Although the ideas expressed above arise from my experience in the UK and in terms of research in education, I suspect that they are applicable in many countries around the world and probably across many of the other areas of social science.

2. SIGNIFICANT INSIGHTS IN RESEARCH IN EDUCATION

I have suggested that 'adventurousness in the choice of topic' is an important criterion of quality in research. What topics might score highly on this criterion, and lead to significant insights that might change the world for the better in some theoretical, or practical, or policy-making way?

(a) Creating academic learning cultures

Most educational researchers focus their research energies onto aspects of the organising, teaching and learning processes of schools, colleges and universities. Certainly, there are many important issues to be addressed in the context of formal education systems. One that I consider has been more or less neglected is described here.

There is a simple, and usually wrong, assumption in society at large and often in schools, colleges, and universities, that if children and students do not learn all that they are taught, it is because they are lazy or stupid. Often, of course, the judgement is expressed in more esoteric language. It is likely however that close observation of children or students who are so labelled will show that they are active and clever about things that really matter to themselves. A more probable explanation of why they do not learn all that they are taught is that they are bored. Certainly that is often their own comment and it is too easy to sweep this away as a vague, ill-defined term covering a range of states of mind. Perhaps a useful metaphor is 'switched off' and this raises the question, 'How can learners be switched on?' It may be that the patterns of schooling, the fragmentation of learning, the usual teaching styles, and the expected learning styles, all contribute to ennui for many learners, but one of the most obviously neglected features of learning communities is the power, for better or worse, of peer pressure. When professors congregate they usually tell each other that education is worthwhile and to be enjoyed. When children and students are together they usually tell each other that education is something to endure, not to enthuse over. The evidence is common knowledge. How do most groups of children or students treat one of themselves that spends longer than the rest at study, or that expresses enthusiasm for academic work?

How can academic learning cultures be created in groups of learners whereby they come to value the endeavours of their peers and positively reinforce each others' learning? This is a topic which merits the combined efforts of many researchers working in teams. It would be an adventurous topic which could be expected to lead to significant insights

This would need the theoretical understandings of social psychologists and the skills of experienced teachers engaging in action research in their own classrooms. It would need effective leadership in order to co-ordinate the efforts, ample resources to enable the researchers to enquire effectively, to meet each other and exchange ideas, and, when and if they come up with some ways forward, extensive support so that the findings could be disseminated widely.

(b) Learning about and beginning to live by intermediate technology

Beyond the type of formal education issue outlined above, there are great societal issues which fundamentally come down to education and the need for thorough research to underpin that education. There are perhaps six billion people on planet Earth. How can they learn to avoid the potential disasters that are associated with famine, environmental pollution, over-population, resource exhaustion, extinction of wild-life species, and ecological disruption? How can they learn to stop racial hatred, ethnic cleansing, genocide? How can they learn to use medical knowledge to reduce the incidence of disease? How can they learn how to organise their political affairs so that the democratic ideal of the open society can prosper? How can they learn to turn growth economics into steady-state economics?

These are educational problems. They require educational research which underpins the judgements and decisions entailed in responding to these educational problems. They should be on the research agenda of university departments of education throughout the world. Intermediate technology is one example.

Chapter Nine ON TRIVIAL PURSUITS AND SIGNIFICANT INSIGHTS

In 1994 I had the privilege of attending the opening ceremony of an environmental education centre at Rantasalmi in eastern Finland. In conveying greetings and best wishes, I said this.

> I wish to say something about the importance of this Centre and of its educational significance.
>
> Trees and lakes are prominent in your environment. Let me talk for a moment about deciduous trees like the birch. There is much to learn from such trees and I would that our political leaders throughout the world, and their political advisers would take time out to think about them. If they would do this, they might reflect on the way in which the frail shoot rising from the seed turns into a slender sapling, which continues to grow upwards until as a mature young tree it reaches its full height. Over the following years it will no longer grow taller but year by year will slowly thicken to become a gnarled but majestic knight of the forest. What I want politicians and economists to realise is that once it has grown to its optimum height from the ground it does not wither or die, but continues to thrive for many many years. In this lies an important metaphor for the growth of economies. The conventional wisdom is that if an economy doesn't grow it will decline. What politicians and economists must learn is how to organise the affairs of our complicated nations as though they were the deciduous trees. We need economies that can be sustained without growth when they have reached maturity. We also need economies that can harmonise with the seasons of the year (as do the trees and everything else in nature except industrial women and men).
>
> My home is in the village of Kirklington in the county of Nottinghamshire in England. People have lived in Kirklington for at least a 1000 years: we know that there was a Saxon community and that they built a water mill to grind corn. I want to tell you about one of its inhabitants of the last century.
>
> He is an unknown Englishman, a man whose name has not been publicly uttered since he was buried in 1898 in the village churchyard. His name was Benjamin Drabble and he lived all his life in Kirklington. He was born in 1818, married a wife called Elizabeth, had six children, and died aged 79. Apart from entries in the church register, census returns, and a few fragments of clay pipes which he smoked, he has left no trace.
>
> Ben Drabble and his family lived in part of the house that now belongs to my family - and this was the starting point of my interest in thinking about him and imagining what his life style was like. He and Elizabeth and their children lived in three rooms - two downstairs and a sleeping loft above reached by a trap door ladder. They had about a quarter acre of land around the cottage. At the back they kept chickens and perhaps occasionally a pig. In the front in long rows of tilled earth they grew potatoes, carrots, parsnips, turnips, leeks, onions, cabbage, cauliflower, Brussels sprouts, lettuce, and perhaps radishes.

Ben worked on the land. He could plough, sow, and reap using a horse sometimes but mostly nothing more than his own muscles. He could build fences, lay hedges, dig ditches, drain fields, fell trees, saw timber. Six days a week he worked from dawn to dusk and on the seventh day he put on his best clothes and went with Elizabeth and the children to church in the morning and in the afternoon smoked his clay pipe, played games with the children, and later grandchildren, and fell asleep in a comfy chair. He worked on the estates of Kirklington Hall and would have had few days of holiday in the year, but we can imagine that sometimes as a young man he might have spent one of those days walking ten miles to Newark to go to the market, and other times he must have walked in the opposite direction to the village of Pinxton , from whence came his bride.

Ben couldn't have earned much as an agricultural labourer, but it would have been enough for Elizabeth to buy things like sugar, tea, and candles from the village store and perhaps a few pints of ale from time to time. Probably they got milk and butter from the farm where he worked and flour by the sack from the water mill nearby. Water came from a well just behind the cottage. The earth privy would have been emptied regularly onto the vegetable garden to enrich the soil. The range, which warmed the living room and on which the food was cooked and water heated for the occasional bath, might have used Nottinghamshire coal or more probably logs from the estate. Of a winter evening they lit an oil lamp, or burned a few candles.

Perhaps you can guess why I am telling you this! My unknown Englishman was an environmental hero. Benjamin Drabble and his family, like the other families of Kirklington at the time and previously, and like many families throughout the non-industrial world now, lived in close relation to the local environment. Nearly everything that they owned and used, originated from within two kilometres of their cottage. By contrast my family draws its sustenance from the four corners of the Earth. We have apples and lamb from New Zealand, beef from South America, wheat from Canada, strawberries from Spain, melons from Israel. We have two cars - one from Italy, one from France. Many of our electronic gadgets come from the Pacific basin. When we travel, again the whole Earth is open to us - in less than a day we can be on the other side of the world. Of course I don't want to decry our life style, like everybody else I enjoy it. But I also sense that we are demanding too much of our environment.

Two men were watching an enormous harvester, one of these computer controlled machines that are used in your forest to cut down trees in a few seconds, weigh the wood and send a radio message back to base telling how much usable timber it has yielded. One of the watchers said, 'But for that machine there would be work for a hundred men with chain saws.' His companion grinned and replied, 'Or a hundred thousand with penknives'.

Chapter Nine ON TRIVIAL PURSUITS AND SIGNIFICANT INSIGHTS

> Somewhere between the life style of Ben Drabble and that of industrial people of today we need to find the right balance. I believe it can only come from a proper understanding of the delicate relationship between human beings and our environment. I am hopeful that here in Finland, tempered by the environmental knowledge that comes from your trees and lakes and harsh winters, you can offer the next generation some wisdom.
>
> That is why this Centre is important. I hope these are messages that you can give to Europe and to the world. I wish you good fortune. Kittos.

This may not be the message or style expected of an educational researcher. I suggest that it should be. The research question is this: What experiences may predispose people to adopt and act on the values of intermediate technology? ['Intermediate technology' is a term coined by Schumacher (1973) to describe something between primitive technology which provides a bare subsistence level of living for its users, and high technology which overconsumes the Earth's resources, pollutes the environment, and disenfranchises most of its users while giving special power to an elite. Schumacher also called it 'technology with a human face'.]

It is important to assert that this issue is about learning and therefore entails research into how the learning takes place and how it can be facilitated. How do some people learn to accept these values but others not? This is a research question for social psychologists and sociologists. How can educators enable people to learn these values? What teaching and learning strategies are helpful? These are questions for educational researchers.

Clearly research into such an issue is a political act which is intensely value-laden. It is preparing the way for a future society which might be economically sustainable for a long period - unlike our present situation. It is using research as a tool for creating a better world.

ENDPIECE

Many years ago, when I was appointed Reader in Education at what was then Trent Polytechnic, I went to the local Director of Education (who was responsible for about 500 schools and colleges) and asked him what educational research we could carry out from the Polytechnic that would be helpful to him. His answer was brief: 'I don't use research, I just play my hunches.'

Playing hunches is certainly one way of creating education: using intuition without challenge and without monitoring the consequences. I guess most of us work this way sometimes, and perhaps some use it all the time.

A second way of creating education is the historical way. It entails repeating what has been done before: basing today's action on the way it was done last week or last year. Again I guess that most of us work this way sometimes, arguing that there is no opportunity to do otherwise. Of course those who haven't done it before, can't use this approach, unless they can hear about and adopt somebody else's experience.

There is a third way. It is creating education by asking questions and searching for evidence. It is creating education by challenging and developing one's own personal theories of education - by asking 'how do I improve my practice?' and 'how do I help you improve your learning?' It is creating education by asking about intentions, by determining their worth, by appraising resources, by identifying alternative strategies, and by monitoring and evaluating outcomes. It is creating education through systematic and critical enquiry. It is creating education through research.

Reader, I hear you mutter that research is slow and time-consuming and expensive. I agree, but nevertheless I seek your agreement that significant research is the potent way forward. Creating education through significant research is the effective way of creating education, and this is something which educational researchers have to keep telling practitioners and policy-makers. In the past there has been too much slavish repetition in education, following the historical model; today there is too much blind playing of hunches in education by politicians in a hurry. For tomorrow we need more recognition of the power of research in creating worthwhile education and of the potential of worthwhile education for creating a better world.

What needs to be done by the community of researchers in education?

First, we need to recognise and respect the fact that research in education is a broad church.

We need to respect the diversity of valid and worthwhile possibilities that coexist in the social sciences in general and research in education in particular. In Chapter One are described the topography and deep structure of the social sciences in terms of realms, categories, kinds of enquiry, audiences, paradigms and ethical values.

In Chapter Three are defined different types of research in education - clearly separating educational research from sociological, psychological, historical and philosophical research in education. It is particularly important that educational research be recognised as research that aims critically to inform educational judgements and decisions in order to improve educational action, while sociological, psychological, historical and philosophical research in education are concerned critically to inform understandings of discipline-pertinent phenomena in educational settings.

Another feature of this broad church is that there are 'insider' and 'outsider' researchers and both play important roles. The insiders are the teachers and administrators in schools, colleges and universities who undertake research into their own practices and policies. The outsiders are the staff of universities and of research institutes who research into the practices and policies of others. Research by insiders is an important way of challenging and improving local practices and policies. It offers high levels of insight into local issues, but may be low on objectivity. Research by outsiders may offer less insight, but more objectivity. However, as I have argued, perhaps research by outsiders, being a scarce resource, should best be directed towards national and global issues.

It is damaging to the whole enterprise of research for the devotees of one sect in this broad church to attack another sect and claim that they alone have seen the light. Mutual respect based on acceptance of differences is vital.

Secondly, we need to raise the quality of research in education.

In Chapter Eight are suggested three prime indications of quality: adventurousness in the choice of topic, elegance in the process of enquiry, and worthwhileness of the product.

Adventurousness in research implies that it may change the world of action or the world of ideas in some significant way: theoretically, practically or policy-wise.

Elegance of the process of enquiry entails a long list of expectations, including quality in: the framing of the research questions which define the purpose of the enquiry, and the reformulation of these as circumstances change; the appropriateness of the rationale or theory which underpins the enquiry; the choice of setting and definition of the boundary if the enquiry is a study of a singularity; the representativeness of the sample if the enquiry is a search for generalisation; the way in which data is systematically recorded, stored, and is potentially available for audit; the extent to which the data are perceived as trustworthy, and are as accurate as necessary; the extent to which the interpretations, explanations and conclusions arise logically and rationally from analysis of the data; the ethics of the enquiry; the extent to which the researchers have been self-critical of their methods and through this have improved the value of their findings; the extent to which the researchers have developed and justified new methods of enquiry; the clarity and lucidity with which the account of the research and its claim to knowledge are expressed; the way in which the empirical conclusion is rigorously framed and then related to similar situations (in a study of a singularity); the way in which the empirical conclusion is rigorously framed in relation to both the sample and the general population (in a search for generalisation); and the extent to which as wide an audience as may benefit from the new knowledge will have the opportunity of access to the publication.

Worthwhileness of the product implies that the research has said something significant, such as challenging existing theory, offering novel insights of potential power, or integrating previously fragmented understandings.

Thirdly, we need to educate ourselves and our students to be skilful in the processes of research and committed to the search for excellence; also we need to teach everybody of the value of research as a tool of democracy

Important as it is that we engage in significant research it is also vital that we sharpen our own skills (for example, the skills of writing lucid research reports), and ensure that there will be an abundance of competent and committed educational researchers in the future. In the United Kingdom at present there are worries about the future supply of educational researchers. Is this also the case elsewhere? Every country needs sufficient people competent to conduct quality research in education.

Beyond that we should strive to ensure that the education of everyone at large is such that, when someone insists 'This is what should be done', people ask 'What is the evidence that this is worthwhile?' Education in a democracy should embrace the importance of research as a vital tool of an open society.

Fourthly, we need to recognise, celebrate and make manifest the power of research for effecting worthwhile change, nationally and globally.

As researchers we have the potential for making the world a better place. Research in education needs to eschew trivial pursuits and instead tackle significant issues about learning which are of national and global importance. Country by country the formal education systems of the world deserve the focused intelligence of researchers striving to improve theory, policy and practice. Globally the world has a need for empirical, reflective and creative research into learning how to prevent famine, war, environmental pollution, over-population, resource depletion, extinction of wild-life species, and disruption of ecological systems.

Creating education through research is not just the title of a book, it is an imperative for democratic societies in a free world.

REFERENCES

Abbott D, Broadfoot P, Croll P, Osborn M and Pollard A (1994)	Some sink, some float: national curriculum assessment and accountability, *British Educational Research Journal* 20(2) 155-174
Adelman C, Jenkins D and Kemmis S (1980)	Rethinking case study: notes from the second Cambridge conference, in Simons H (1980)
Alexander R, Rose J and Woodhead C (1992)	*Curriculum Organisation and Practice in Primary Schools: a discussion document,* Department of Education and Science, London, HMSO
Ausubel D P and Robinson F G (1971)	*School Learning: an Introduction to Educational Psychology,* London, Holt Rinehart and Winston
Ball S J (1990)	*Politics and Policy Making in Education,* London, Routledge
Barnes D (1969)	Language, the learner and the school: see Entwistle and Nisbet (1972)
Barker Lunn J C (1970)	Streaming in the primary school and Attitudes of pupils: see Entwistle and Nisbet (1972)
Bassey M (1978)	*Nine Hundred Primary School Teachers,* Windsor, England, NFER Publishing Company
Bassey M (1980)	Crocodiles eat children, *Bulletin of Classroom Action Research Network* (1980)
Bassey M (1981)	Pedagogic research: on the relative merits of search for generalisation and study of single events, *Oxford Review of Education,* 7(1) 73-94
Bassey M (1992a)	Creating education through research, *British Educational Research Journal,* 18(1) 3-16
Bassey M (1992b)	*The Great Education Conspiracy?* London, Local Education Authority Publications (LEAP)
Bassey M (1994)	Why Lord Skidelsky is so wrong, *The Times Educational Supplement* (21 January)
Beard R M, Bligh D A and Harding A G (1978)	*Research into Teaching Methods in Higher Education* (4th edition), Surrey, England, Society for Research into Higher Education
Bell J F (1990)	The curriculum for English 15-year-old pupils in 1984, *British Educational Research Journal* 16(1) 41-52
Bennett N (1976)	*Teaching Styles and Pupil Progress,* London, Open Books
Bennett N (1992)	*Managing Learning in Classrooms,* Stoke-on-Trent, Trentham Books

Bligh D A (1971)	*What's the Use of Lectures?* London University, University Teaching Methods Unit
British Educational Research Association (1992)	*Ethical Guidelines for Educational Research,* Edinburgh, BERA
Britton J N, Martin N C and Rosen H (1966)	Multiple marking of English composition: see Entwistle and Nisbet (1972)
Busby S (1991)	The management of children in the dining room at lunch-time, in Lomax, P (ed) *Managing better schools and colleges: an action research way,* BERA Dialogues, Clevedon, England, Multilingual Matters
Butcher H J (ed) (1968)	*Educational Research in Britain* (vol 1) University of London Press
Cane B S and Schroeder C (1970)	The teacher and research: see Entwistle and Nisbet (1972)
Cohen L (1976)	*Educational Research in Classrooms and Schools,* London, Harper and Row
Cohen L and Manion L (1980, 1989)	*Research Methods in Education,* London, Croom Helm
Collinson D, Kirkup G, Kyd R and Slocombe L (1992)	*Plain English,* Buckingham, Open University Press
Deem R, Brehony K and Heath S (1994)	Governors, schools and the miasma of the market, *British Educational Research Journal* 20(5) 535-549
Department of Education and Science (1967)	*Children and their Primary Schools: a Report for the Central Advisory Council for Education* (Plowden Report) London, HMSO
Douglas J W B, Ross J M and Simpson H R (1968)	All our future: see Entwistle and Nisbet (1972)
Economic and Social Research Council (1991)	*Postgraduate Training Guidelines,* Swindon, ESRC
Eggleston J (1979)	The characteristics of educational research: mapping the domain, *British Educational Research Journal* 5(1) 1-12
Entwistle N J (1973)	*The Nature of Educational Research,* Milton Keynes, Open University Press
Entwistle N J and Nisbet J D (1972)	*Educational Research in Action,* London, Hodder and Stoughton
Fleming W G (1986)	The interview: a neglected issue in research on student learning, *Higher Education* 15(5)
Ford J (1969)	Making friends at school: see Entwistle and Nisbet (1972)

REFERENCES

Fowler H W (1926, 1965)	*A Dictionary of Modern English Usage,* London, Oxford University Press
Fraser E D (1969)	Home environment and the school: see Entwistle and Nisbet (1972)
Hammersley M and Scarth J (1993)	Beware of Wise Men Bearing Gifts: a case study in the misuse of educational research, *British Educational Research Journal,* 19(5) 489-498
Hasan P and Butcher H J (1966)	Creativity and intelligence: see Entwistle and Nisbet (1972)
Illich I (1973)	*Tools for Conviviality,* London, Calder and Boyars
Jeffreys M V C (1950)	*Glaucon: an Enquiry into the Aims of Education,* London, Pitman
Keeves J P (ed) (1988)	*Educational Research, Methodology and Measurement: an International Handbook,* Oxford, Pergamon Press
Kerslake D (1982)	Talking about mathematics, in Torbe, M (ed) *Language teaching and learning Vol 6 Mathematics,* London, Ward Locke Educational
Keys W and Fernandes C (1993)	*What do Students think about School?* Berkshire, National Foundation for Educational Research
Lewis A (1992)	Group child interviews as a research tool, *British Educational Research Journal* 18(4) 413-421
Lerman S (1990)	Alternative perspectives of the nature of mathematics and their influence on the teaching of mathematics, *British Educational Research Journal* 16(1) 53-61
Maclure M (1993)	Arguing for yourself: identity as an organising principle in teachers' jobs and lives, *British Educational Research Journal* 19(4) 311-322
Maccoby E E and Jacklin C N (1974)	*The Psychology of Sex Differences,* California, Stanford University Press
Morton-Williams R and French S (1968)	Schools Council Enquiry 1 - young school leavers: see Entwistle and Nisbet (1972)
National Commission on Education (1993)	*Learning to Succeed,* London, Heinemann
Nisbet J D (1974)	Educational research: the state of the art, in Dockerell W B and Hamilton D (1980) (eds) *Rethinking Educational Research,* London, Hodder and Stoughton
Nisbet J D and Entwistle N J (1972)	*Educational Research Methods,* London, Hodder and Stoughton

Nisbet J D and Welsh J (1972)	A local evaluation of primary school French: see Entwistle and Nisbet (1972)
Osborn A F and Milbank J E (1987)	*The Effects of Early Education: a Report from the Child Health and Education Study,* London, Oxford University Press
Paechter C (1993)	What happens when a school subject undergoes a sudden change of status? *Curriculum Studies* 1(3) 349-363
Pajares M F (1992)	Teachers' Beliefs and Educational Research: Cleaning Up a Messy Construct, *Review of Educational Research* 62, 3, 307-332
Peaker G F (1967)	The regression analyses of the national survey: see Entwistle and Nisbet (1972)
Perry W G (1978)	Sharing the Costs of Growth, in Parker C A (ed) *Encouraging Development in College Students*
Peters R S (1966)	*Ethics and Education,* London, George Allen and Unwin
Peters R S and White J P (1969)	The philosopher's contribution to educational research, in: Taylor W (ed) *Research Perspectives in Education,* London, Routledge and Kegan Paul
Plewis I (1991)	Underachievement: a case of conceptual confusion, *British Educational Research Journal* 17(4) 377-385
Ranson S (1992)	*The Management and Organisation of Educational Research,* Swindon, Economic and Social Research Council
Richards P N and Bolton N (1971)	Types of mathematics teaching, mathematical ability and divergent thinking in junior school children: see Entwistle and Nisbet (1972)
Riseborough G F (1994)	Teachers careers and comprehensive school closure: policy and professionalism in practice, *British Educational Research Journal* 20(1) 85-104
Rosenshine B and Furst N (1973)	The use of direct observation to study teaching, in Travers R M W (ed)
Rushworth L (1993)	The implementation and evaluation of a drama course for all secondary pupils in a comprehensive school, in Turner D (ed) *Research in action,* Pavic Publications, Sheffield
Schumacher E F (1973)	*Small is Beautiful: a Study of Economics as though People Mattered,* London, Blond and Briggs
Short G (1994)	Teaching about the holocaust: a consideration of some ethical and pedagogic issues, *Educational Studies* 20(1) 53-67
Simon B (1978)	Educational Research: Which Way? *British Educational Research Journal* 4(1) 2-7
Simon B (1985)	*Does Education Matter?,* London, Lawrence and Wishart

REFERENCES

Simons H (Ed) (1980) — *Towards a Science of the Singular* Norwich, CARE, University of East Anglia

Skidelsky Lord (1993) — *Hansard,* 7 December col 882-883

Stenhouse L (1975) — *An Introduction to Curriculum Research and Development,* London, Heinemann

Stenhouse L (1978) — Case study and case records: towards a contemporary history of education, *British Educational Research Journal* 4(2) 21-39

Stenhouse L (1980) — The study of samples and the study of cases, *British Educational Research Journal* 6(1) 1-6

Stones E (1979) — *Psychopedagogy,* London, Methuen

Todman J and Lawrenson H (1992) — Computer anxiety in primary schoolchildren and university students, *British Educational Research Journal* 18(1) 63-72

Tolkein J R R (1954, 1966) — *The Lord of the Rings,* London, George Allen and Unwin

Travers R M W (ed) (1973) — *Second Handbook of Research on Teaching,* Chicago, Rand McNally

Tripp D (1993) — *Critical Incidents in Teaching,* London, Routledge

Vernon P E (1971) — Effects of administration and scoring on divergent thinking tests: see Entwistle and Nisbet (1972)

Wiliam D (1992) — Value-added attacks: technical issues in reporting national curriculum, *British Educational Research Journal* 18(4) 329-341

Williams A (1993) — Teacher perceptions of their needs as mentors in the context of developing school-based initial teacher education, *British Educational Research Journal* 19(4) 407-420

Williams J D (1969) — Educational research, in *Blond's Encyclopaedia of Education,* London, Blond Educational

Williams K (1976) — Cartoon in *The Times Higher Education Supplement* 26 November

Wragg E C (1970) — Interaction analysis as a feedback system for student teachers: see Entwistle and Nisbet (1972)

Wright S (1990) — Language counts in the teaching of mathematics, in Webb, R (ed) *Practitioner research in the primary school,* Basingstoke, Falmer Press

Young M (1958) — *The Rise of the Meritocracy,* London, Thames and Hudson

NAMES INDEX

Abbott D 40, 113
Adelman C 111
Alexander R 30
Ausubel D P 95
Ball S 22-26
Barker Lunn J C 93
Barnes D 91
Beard R M 100
Bell J F 46, 116
Bennett N 34, 101
Bligh D A 100
Bolton N 91
Brehony K 43, 114
Britton J N 92
Broadfoot P 40, 113
Busby S 47, 115
Butcher H J 36, 93
Cane B S 94
Cohen L 88, 96, 111
Collinson D 84
Croll P 40, 113
Deem R 43, 114
Drabble B 135
Douglas J W B 92
Eggleston J 88
Elliott J 46
Entwistle N 36
Entwistle N 36, 90, 95, 99
Fernandes C 106, 113, 117
Fleming W G 15
Ford J 94
Fowler H W 84
Fraser E D 92
French S 93
Furst N 99
Gower E 84
Hamilton D 112
Hammersley M 30, 31
Harding A G 100
Hasan P 93
Heath S 43, 114
Illich I 20
Jacklin C N 89
Jeffreys M V C 20
Jenkins D 111
Keeves J P 87
Kemmis S 111
Keys W 106, 113, 117
Kerslake D 53
Kirkup G 84
Kyd R 84
Lawrenson H 45, 115
Lerman S 46, 117
Lewis A 41, 114

Lomax P 47, 115
Maccoby E E 89
Maclure M 44, 115
Manion L 88, 111
Martin N C 92
Milbank J E 83, 103, 113, 116
Morton-Williams R 93
Nisbet J D 36, 88, 90, 94, 95
Osborn A F 83, 103, 113, 116
Osborn M 40, 113
Paechter C 43, 117
Pajares M F 28
Peaker G F 92
Peters R S 21, 36
Plewis I 42, 117
Pollard A 40, 113
Ranson S 24, 29
Richards P N 91
Riseborough G F 42, 114
Robinson F G 95
Rose J 30
Rosen H 92
Rosenshine B 99
Ross J M 92
Rushworth L 48, 115
Scarth J 30, 31
Schon D 34
Schroeder C 94
Schumacher E F 20, 137
Short G 40, 114
Simon B 24, 36, 38
Simons H 87, 112
Simpson H R 92
Skidelsky 33-35, 52, 87
Slocombe L 84
Stenhouse L 2, 9, 38, 88
Stones E 88
Todman J 45, 115
Tolkein J R R 84
Travers R M W 99
Tripp D 38, 39
Turner D 48, 115
Vernon P E 94
Webb R 49, 116
Welsh J 94
White J P 36
Wiliam D 41, 117
Williams A 41, 114
Williams J D 36
Williams K 33
Woodhead C 30
Wragg E C 91
Wright S 49, 51, 116
Young M 24

SUBJECT INDEX

Academic mode of reporting research 64
Action research 6, 46; some examples 47 et seq
Adventurousness in research: a criterion of quality 119, 144
Audiences for research findings 9
Authors per academic paper in RAE of 1992 130
Beliefs in relation to research 28
Broad church - research in education is a, 143
Case study 111
Claim to knowledge in a research paper 71
Closed generalisation 97
Common-sense theory 57
Communication - formal dissemination level of, 10
Communication - informal interactive level of, 10
Communication - personal level of, 10
Competitive elitists: an ideological group 27
Conceptual background as theoretical basis of research 57, 73
Conviviality 20
Creating academic learning cultures 133
Creative research: one of three realms of research 5
Critique of a research paper - a framework of questions for making a, 68
Cultural restorationists: an ideological group 26
Cyclical research 59
Data analysing and interpreting 59
Data collection 58
Democracy - research as a tool of, 144
Discourse of derision 22
Drabble, Ben, agricultural labourer 135
Education - suggested definition of, 20
Educational action research 46 et seq
Educational research - suggested definition of, 40
Elegance of the process of enquiry: a criterion of quality 120, 144
Empirical generalisations 97
Empirical research reports - writing of, 69
Empirical research: one of three realms of research 5
ESRC Postgraduate Training Guidelines 37
Ethics: respect for democratic values 16
Ethics: respect for persons 15
Ethics: respect for truth 16
Evaluative research 6
Fields of study of research in education: RAE (1992) 129
Flaws and fripperies in research writing 76 et seq
Funding of research in the UK 127
Generalisations 7, 97
Genuflection: a frippery 77
Harvard system - referencing by, 80
Hiding the instruments: a frippery 78
Historical research in education 45
Industrial trainers: an ideological group 26
Insiders and outsiders 6, 143
Intermediate technology 134, 137
Interpretive research paradigm 13
Intervention and non-intervention studies 59
Kingmaking: a frippery 77
Knowledge - a simple description of kinds of, 3
Linear research 59

Local jargon: a frippery 78
Making a claim to knowledge 59
Meritocracy 24
Murgatroyd's day: examples of positivist and interpretive data 14
Narrative reporting (as different from structured reporting) 67
Nature of reality 11
Normative generalisations 97
Not statistically significant but...: a flaw 78
Numbered notes - referencing by, 81
Opaqueness: a flaw 77
Open generalisation 97
Over-crunching numbers: a flaw 78
Over-generalising: a flaw 79
Paradigm - meaning of, 12
Pedagogic mode of reporting research 65
Personal and impersonal styles of writing 67
Planning of research - questions to guide the, 61
Politicians: different from researchers 22
Positivist research paradigm 12
Potential abstract: a tool for planning 62
Professional mode of reporting research 65
Progressives: an ideological group 25
Psychological research in education - suggested definition of, 44
Publication record of a university department of education - a fictional example of a, 130
Quality of research in education 119 et seq
Rantasalmi Environmental Education Centre, Finland - opening of, 135
Rational progressives: an ideological group 27
Referencing the literature 79
Reflective research papers - writing of, 82
Reflective research: one of three realms of research 5
Reflective studies: some examples 117
Research assessment exercise of UK HEFC in 1992 127
Research hypothesis 55
Research issue 55
Research problem 55
Research questions, in relation to issues, problems and hypotheses 54
Respect for democratic values 16
Respect for persons 15
Respect for truth 16
Sandbagging: a frippery 77
Search for generalisation 7, 87 et seq; examples 116 et seq
Significant insights in research 128
Singularity, concept of a 7, 110 et seq
Sociological research in education - suggested definition of, 42
Study of a singularity 7, 110; examples 113 et seq
Structured reporting (as different from narrative reporting) 66
Suppression of minorities: a flaw 79
Theoretical research 6
Theory-in-the-literature 57
Title - the last stage of research writing is devising of a, 76
Traditionalists: an ideological group 25
Trivial pursuits in research 128
Uncertain claim to knowledge: a flaw 77
Use of the first person 67
Worthwhile culture (in a framework definition of education) 20
Worthwhile living (in a framework definition of education) 20
Worthwhileness of the product - a criterion of quality 121, 144